DARE TO BELIEVE

DARE TO BELIEVE

12 Lessons for Living Your Soul Purpose

Jessica Joines

Dare to Believe

Copyright © 2018 Jessica Joines

For permission requests, write to: info@jessicajoines.com

Cover by Josh Namdar.
Edited by Jasmine Dilmanian aka Wordie.
Interior Layout by Sandeep Likhar.

ISBN: 978-0-578-42001-1 (paperback)
ISBN: 978-0-578-42000-4 (eBook)

Printed in the United States of America.
First printed November 2018.
Library of Congress Control Number: 2018964442
Published by Divinely True Publishing. www.DivinelyTrue.com

For Cadie and Levi.

May you each live your soul purpose every day of your life.

Contents

Preface

This is your moment.

Your moment to move beyond what's been.

To flourish.

To feel pure joy.

Now is your time.

Going through the motions stops now.

Being unfulfilled stops now.

Wondering *what if* stops. Now.

This is your moment.

As we embark on this journey together (one cannot do it alone), I ask you to practice letting go. Let go of everything you've told yourself up to this point in your life. The negative thoughts, fears, and self-doubt—they are no longer yours to cradle.

Now, take a deep breath in.

As you breathe out, simply release.

And again.

Now, we're ready to start. Consciously open your heart and allow this truth to enter:

> *You have a purpose that is especially and wholly unique to you. It's what you came here to do. Your purpose fills your soul in a way that you have only dreamed about, but never believed possible–until now.*
>
> *Know this: You were born to live your soul purpose. Like the instincts to eat and breathe, your soul purpose is innate to your being. It is key*

to everything that is possible for you. It is your happiness. And at this crossroads, the whole world is waiting for you to start living it. Your journey begins now.

Are you ready? Let's do this.

Note to the Collective Self

Now is the time when we reject the inner voice that tells us what we truly want is impossible. Those secret dreams that are hidden deep within our hearts. The ones about the life we've always wanted, but for too long have shut down, disregarded, and outright ignored.

Now, is the time.

We come together to affirm the truth we've always known—that we were never meant to be working each day doing something we don't love or living lives that don't fully resonate with our souls. To this we no longer subscribe.

We're shedding the negative beliefs around lack and limitation that have been holding us back. We're letting go of everything within us and outside of us that has told us our destiny is anything other than happiness. And, we're silencing the inner voice that tells us our deepest desires are nothing more than a pipe dream.

We're transforming the collective consciousness.

What resides within our hearts is no longer impossible, irresponsible, unrealistic, or selfish. Those illusions are being dissolved, permanently and completely.

We know we are here for a higher purpose. No matter how humble or big, our life's work is our passion. We no longer wish to *just* get by or survive. We choose abundance.

We affirm that we are living in a world that is happening *for* us, not *to* us. Fear is no longer our controller. Our decisions, choices, and actions are anchored in love.

Will it always be easy? No.

Will there be moments when we want to give up? Yes. However, we embrace change and welcome our vulnerability.

With our collective will to believe, we are entering a new paradigm. We pursue soul purpose because we know it is the key to our awakened consciousness.

This is why we dare to believe.

A Love Letter

Long before I learned about love, my world was mostly one of pain, self-sabotage, and sadness. Loneliness and fear were all I could feel. After years of being numb and feeling helpless, I harnessed the fear of never getting what I really wanted and turned it around to make a life-altering decision: to *dare to believe* in a better possibility for my life. In doing so, I had to let go of the fears that plagued me. And, begin a path of self-love.

No longer did I want to live in world where I was the victim. No longer did I want to feel powerless over my circumstances, or alcohol, and as a result, the destiny of my dreams. I wanted to feel, anything, especially love. I wanted to be one of *those* people. You know, the ones who wake up excited and happy about their day. Living lives they love—courageously following their dreams. Not hiding in their apartments, alone, with empty bottles and tear stained pillow sheets. This was me.

Every. Single. Day. I used to wake up in debilitating fear. Sometimes, I wasn't sure I wanted to continue waking. This was me; endless years, days and countless minutes, in pain. It knew no bounds; my fear. My relationship with suffering is an intimate one. I remember many times endlessly begging for "God" (if he even really existed) to ease my pain; by whatever means necessary. It was as if I believed my life was being decided by the fickle impulses of an unforgiving universe, to which I begged for mercy. As if God were a whimsical genie—a power outside of me.

At first, the root of my pain was just the longing to be free from *it*. The thing that seemed to control my life: fear. I'd later come to realize it as a self-induced imprisonment. I, not *it*, was the one constant. But that wasn't something I could yet see. I had to change my perspective first. And, I had to surrender.

Luckily, those dark times feel like a long time ago. Sometimes it seems like another lifetime and person all together. But it was and is still a part of me, despite a lot of healing. In fact, that self-destructive voice is still there. I can hear her. Laced with self-doubt, fear, and second-guessing. She still likes to visit, though she does so less often.

When she does come along, it's always under the guise of *weighing in* on what I'm doing. A helpful opinion, if you will. It's always about something she's afraid of, things she questions, or things she simply doesn't like. Of course, it comes off like she has my best interest at heart. Because, she does, in her own way.

However, the voice of my toughest critic—my ego self—always quiets and cowers when I look her directly in the eye, with all the force that I have, and tell her that I love her. That catches her off guard. It is usually then that she disappears. I've come to realize that's what happens when you turn on the light.

For this reason, that darker part of me, my ego self, gets a love letter from me often. It helps to keep *her* at bay, when she's accepted. In my messages, I tell her how wonderful, valued, and important she is. I tell her how much I respect her, often reminding her of all the ways she's helped me become who *I am*. And even though she presents it otherwise, she likes to feel loved and appreciated.

In my letters, I often have to tell her, ever so gently, that she's not horrible, worthless or stupid. I remind her that her that she's not a bad person despite the things she's done. I try to help her have faith and belief in her dreams—in the great possibility for her life—though sometimes this is better received than others.

At this point in the letter, is usually when she quiets down. That's when I know I have her. When I know she's allowed the love to enter. In fact, here's a letter I wrote to her, my ego self, not too long ago:

Love Letter
3/31/18

Dear Jessica (ego self),

I know you don't want to hear it right now, but I love you. With everything in me, I absolutely, 100% love you.

It's makes me sad when I see you beating yourself up in the way you do. Do you know how painful it is to watch? It's like you're taking a knife and twisting around and around in your heart. So, tell me why. Why do you do it? You are perfect just as you are. Don't you see that? I wish you did.

So listen here, my beloved. I'm writing to remind you that you matter. To me and to everyone you meet; you are loved. I love you. More than you can possibly understand.

In fact, I think you're absolutely beautiful. On the inside and out! You're sensitive and caring. You're powerful. When you talk, people listen. It's almost like when you open your mouth, those around you are healed. It's a gift. You are a gift, my dear. Wholly and completely.

One of the things that I love most about you is that deep down you have this unique way of looking at the world. Your compassion and warmth are one-of-a-kind. You're wise, sensitive, witty and you have an uncanny sense of humor. You're sharp. And sometimes, even a little sarcastic. Especially when you're overly passionate about something. It's something I love most about you.

But hey, listen… I know that deep down, you don't believe in yourself. And while everyone looks at you and sees this incredibly accomplished woman, you actually feel like nothing—worthless—when you are anything but.

So, let's do this. Let's stop the minute-by-minute autocorrect and practice being okay with vulnerability. It's OK to show people who you really are. I promise they will still love you. Don't you know? That's where true strength resides my love. And, you, my dear, have this in spades. You are one of the most courageous and bravest people I know. With all the dozens times you've been knocked down, who else would keep trying like you do? I mean, you just don't give up. No matter what. It's like the world seemingly says NO and instead of cowering in the corner, you say, "I don't believe you!" And you do this over and over again. You are a fighter.

More than anything, I want you to know that I've got your back. You are never alone; despite what you think. I've got you…we've got you.

So take this in! It's YOUR time to shine, my dear one! And, your light is so bright that it's going to blind the world. (Hey world, sunglasses on!)

Know that I love you incredibly and immensely, always and forever. I'm talking about stupid, ridiculous, all-encompassing love!

I am always here with you.

All my love,
Jessica (higher self)

CHAPTER 1

What is Soul Purpose?

*"Be fearless in the pursuit of what sets
your soul on fire"*
- Unknown

Soul purpose is that drive, desire, and inner calling that lights you up and fills you with passion and pure joy. It feeds your soul with such intensity and drive that it *becomes* a spiritual calling. Soul purpose is different than simply *finding* meaning in what you do; as meaning can always be found. What you truly desire to do with your life is something different. It's often aligned to what most needs to be healed, within us.

Soul purpose is not something that can be *figured out*, as no mind on its own can truly know it. That's why no tests or diagrams will reveal it to you. In fact, soul purpose is entirely illogical. It's an inner calling that only your heart knows. When ignited, there is nothing more powerful than the vital force of a heart's desire.

Most people, including myself, can seemingly spend decades of their life not knowing what their calling actually is. Even worse, many have convinced themselves they don't have one; that they're somehow excluded. But once you come to know *it*, it's impossible to ignore. It will dominate you completely. That's because what you're often hearing for the first time are the whispers of your true self. At least, this was the case for me.

I was just looking for a way to be happy. For many years, I saw my job as the source of my pain, and used alcohol to numb it. I thought that if I could just wake up each day and do something I loved, I would no longer be miserable. This is was in part correct, but I've come to realize there's so much more. It's still evolving.

When I finally made myself available to what was in my heart and gave it permission to come forward, I began to step into my soul purpose. As a result, I also came to know my true self, as the fears that had long plagued me, began to subside. That's because stepping into your soul purpose is synonymous with embarking on an alignment to your true self. As it is the true or higher self that holds the secret to our ultimate fulfillment. In fact, it is here, where soul purpose lives.

A True Self Calling

You might be familiar with the concept of the true self. I like how spiritual teacher and author Sue Monk Kidd describes this inner identity[1]. She says the true self is "not our creation, but God's. It is the self we are in our depths. It is our capacity for divinity and transcendence." In other words, it's who you *really* are.

But for so many, like me, it's a part of ourselves that we've long been disconnected from. A part of ourselves that we've ignored or buried. And while many hide their true self for years—even decades—it's always there. When you step into soul purpose living, it is akin to remembering that you are a divine being of love.

A Soul Awakening

For all these reasons and more, you might experience a spiritual awakening as you embark on this journey. When you connect to that thing you love more than anything and feel the power of belief—*in knowing*—that you can do what you love each day, your

---

[1] Sue Monk Kidd, When the Heart Waits, 2006.

consciousness will shift. To experience this, you'll need to open your heart and quiet your mind to hear, or understand, your inner calling. Then, you can begin to align it with your outside world. Eckart Tolle explains the concept of purpose and consciousness a different way when we states: "Even if you achieve your outer purpose, it will never satisfy you if you haven't found your inner purpose, which is awakening, being present, being in alignment with life. True power comes out of the presence; It is the presence[2]." In other words, *living* your soul purpose is synonymous with *becoming awakened.*

Simply put, soul purpose is about awakening to who you really are; an embodiment of heart. Knowing your heart as the real *you* and operating from this place, despite what the world is showing you, is the goal. As while the truth is interconnectedness and love, many of us experience a reality that says otherwise. When we begin to acknowledge and consciously living from this one truth, opposed to the illusion of fear, we are on our way.

I, myself, wasn't setting out to embark on a spiritual journey and perhaps you aren't either. Maybe you just want to get out of a job you hate or be a little less miserable. That was my original intention, too. I wanted to find "my purpose" as a means to ease my pain, and perhaps (if I was lucky), realize my dreams. The unexpected gift was an awakening. I hope it will be yours, too.

A Path, Not a Destination

The initial part of your path to soul purpose can be jarring and confusing at first. Often, when you first come to understand what your heart really wants, the mind will tell you that it's inconvenient, irrational, or impossible. But don't worry, this does subside. Once you work through the fear and doubt, the path will

---

[2] Eckart Tolle, A New Earth, 2005.

become illuminated, one step at a time.

The key for me in this process has been complete and total surrender. When I accepted and then believed in what I once thought was *just* a dream, the magic started to happen. Do you remember the first time you fell in love? There was likely no choice in the matter. There was nothing you could do to not be in love with this person. In fact, it might have hit you like a ton of bricks, and in that moment, you were completely vulnerable to this person. They held your heart in their hands. Soul purpose is surrendering to what you love, plain and simple. When you accept *what* you love as *your* truth, you also deepen your love for *self.*

In this moment, your whole world will open up in a new yet unexpected way. You will start to see color where there was once darkness. Love where there was fear. When you stop trying to push your soul purpose away from you and accept it as you, everything will be different; your perception will change. You'll have hope where once there might have been depression or despair. For me, it was a huge relief. I could finally breathe with the knowledge that I was coming home to the real me.

This is not to say the path isn't going to be met with fear. I still face many fears and doubts. I am not yet free from them. Not by a long shot. I've found that when you spend the majority of your adult life denying your truth, the sources of your unique fears don't just vanish overnight. And when fear has been a primary driver of your existence, a lot of thoughts in your head require excavation.

For me, there are fears of not getting what I want or what I need, being laughed at, and failure. What are all these things about and where do they come from? And how do I no longer let them define me? I practice walking through the fear, consciously choosing love instead.

What I've learned from my own path is that my soul purpose was always there; It had just been hidden in plain view. The more I was able to open my heart and connect to it, the more of my new reality emerged. Later, free from much of the self-imposed restriction and doubt, it began to flourish.

In this book, I share parts of my journey and the spiritual lessons I've developed and practiced that have been essential to my experience of soul purpose. As with everything in life, my inspiration for these lessons is in part from the teachers[3] who have inspired me the most. The ones who have imprinted onto me, via their own divine guidance, my spiritual views about the world. Things like knowing that every moment is an opportunity to choose love and that the great lesson for us all here in "Earth school" is to reject the illusions of fear and separation. As a spiritual student and teacher, the lessons you will experience have been created through applying what I've learned, as well as my own inner, divine guidance and practical usage.

You can be certain that no matter how long you've denied your dreams, either consciously or unconsciously, it's not too late. Further, you can be sure that you have a unique calling—no one is exempt, even though you may have been taught that living your purpose is a rare occurrence. You also may have learned that dreams are difficult to manifest. That they border on fantasy— unrealistic, irrational, and silly. Herein lies the first lesson, which is to *believe* otherwise.

---

[3] Louise Hay, Marianne Williamson, Eckhart Tolle, Oprah Winfrey, Michael Beckwith.

Believe That You Have a Unique Soul Purpose

Why?

Before even understanding what your calling is, it's important that you first believe that you have a unique soul purpose. If you don't, it's hard to accept the reality of yours—to know it. Therefore, the first lesson centers around your assumptions about the concept of a soul purpose. The key is to identify what, if any, core beliefs are holding you back, release them, and allow new ones to enter.

The Practice: Belief Soul Audit

The purpose of a *belief soul audit* is to strengthen your core belief muscle, specifically as it works with soul purpose. Identifying and shedding any belief systems you have around the idea of having a soul purpose is core to the practice. For example, if you believe in the concept of a soul purpose, but that you're somehow excluded, this practice will help you to shift your thinking. Essential to this practice is leveraging visualization and affirmation techniques that serve to shift beliefs stored in both the conscious and subconscious mind. It's best to engage in this practice weekly, until your own intuitive guidance tells you it's no longer needed.

What You'll Need

- A journal to keep track of your weekly practice.
- As with all practices in this book, be sure to date your work and keep a record of your experience with the

practice along with any other pertinent notes. This will help you to reflect upon your progress as needed.

- 10-20 small pieces of paper
- A pen or pencil
- A red marker
- A quiet place that enables you to be fully present

How to Do It

Sitting in a quiet place, without distraction, follow these simple steps:

Step 1: Take a few deep breaths to center yourself and focus your attention.

Step 2: Set the intention to receive everything you need from this exercise through reciting the following aloud:

I call on divine guidance and my higher self to help me receive everything I need from this exercise toward more deeply believing that I have a unique soul purpose. According to divine will and for the highest good. And so it is!

Step 3: First, ask yourself where you currently sit on the belief spectrum about whether you believe that you have a unique, soul purpose, using the chart below as guidance.

Belief Soul Audit

1	2	3	4	5	6
Soul purpose isn't real	Soul purpose is real for others, but not for me	I want to believe but I have serious doubts	I believe more and more...but I still have doubts	I believe, but sometimes my belief falters	I believe I have a unique soul purpose 100% of the time

Step 4: Identify the beliefs that are holding you back from being higher on the scale. Write one belief at a time on a single piece of

small paper. *Examples* of possible beliefs are in the left column below. Feel free to identify any trends you are seeing about possible core belief systems from which your thoughts stem. The right column shows you examples of this.

Be sure to write down any and all beliefs that come to mind, whether or not they are listed in the examples below. There is no magic number.

Stated Belief	Core Belief
My destiny isn't to be rich or abundant.	Fixed destiny
I'm meant to live a life of struggle.	Fixed destiny
Life is supposed to be hard, not easy.	Fixed destiny
Not everyone can be abundant or successful.	Scarcity
If everyone were a celebrity, there would be no celebrities.	Scarcity
Money, love, happiness, etc. are hard to come by.	Scarcity
I need to repent before I can ever step into abundance or true happiness.	Punishing God
Not everyone is worthy enough to live a life of bliss.	Punishing God
I have too much karma to pay back to step into abundance in this lifetime.	Punishing God

Step 5: Compile all of your pieces of paper into a stack and hold them between your palms while saying the following aloud:

I hereby release all of these beliefs from my entire state of being and consciousness. I ask for help in fully releasing these beliefs so that they no longer block me from living my soul purpose. I ask that new, higher vibrational beliefs enter into my consciousness in their place.

If you like working with visualization, imagine these beliefs being swept up in a huge spiral of white light.

Step 6: Next, take your red marker, circle each belief, and put a large X through it. While doing this, really try to feel yourself letting go of these beliefs; intend for them to be released fully and completely. When you are done, you can dispose of the papers.

Step 7: In your journal, write one to two paragraphs that explain why soul purpose exists in your case. Be sure to indirectly address some of the limiting beliefs that were holding you back. Here's an example:

> *I believe that there is a divine soul purpose for me as there is for every person on the planet. This includes a unique life calling, where it's possible to make money doing what makes me happy, every single day. Unlike what I've been told, that life is hard and a struggle, soul purpose is the easiest thing I will ever do. And it will be the most rewarding. Living my soul purpose is my absolute destiny. To think or believe anything else is just an illusion; One that's based in fear.*

When you are finished, feel free to read your paragraph out loud. This will help to strengthen the new belief you've created within you.

Step 8: Thank your higher self and any divine guidance that was present to assist you in your work.

Repeat this process weekly or until you feel a shift in your attitude toward the idea of having a soul purpose. Once the judgment, skepticism and disbelief begin to subside, you'll know you've completed this work.

CHAPTER 2

A Heart-Centered Endeavor

"Being must be felt. It can't be thought."
- Eckart Tolle

Despite what you think, suffering does not have to be your destiny. When you step into the awareness that you don't have to spend your life doing something you don't love, an awakening starts to happen. This is *how* you begin to step into your soul purpose—by shifting your awareness of what's possible. This is how it worked for me.

But how do you uncover your soul purpose? The answer is that you must first embrace your feelings as clues about your truth. Being in touch with the desires that are in your heart is how you come to understand your purpose. That's because soul purpose is something that's centered *entirely* in your heart, not your mind. Have you ever experienced a tough decision that was a war between your heart and your head? Was your heart telling you one thing while your mind was telling you another? Realizing your soul purpose is a lot like that. It's the ultimate head-versus-heart battle you'll experience until you give up and allow your heart to lead.

As a person who has lived most of my life shying away from my heart and instead embracing my mind, it took me a while to believe that my own instincts served as the best guide. From how well I did in school to how intellectual I believed I was, my head had gotten me pretty far in life, which is why leading with the heart felt foreign at first. However, when I remembered the places where my head *alone* had taken me, the choice became easy.

My Battle with Addiction

My road to recovery has been met with many challenges. I began my recovery journey in 2003 but struggled for many years, until I finally surrendered in 2016. I convinced myself that the problems in my 20s that first led me to getting sober were "a phase"—symptoms of other problems, not addiction itself. I didn't understand that when you're an addict, you can trick yourself into thinking just about anything if it means avoiding accepting the truth and its inevitable consequences. For a long time, I believed *the lies* that my mind told me—namely that I wasn't *really* an alcoholic. I was imprisoned by my own insane, delusional thinking. For anyone who's ever battled addiction, you know all too well the tricks your mind can play on you when it comes to this disease. Denial and self-delusion are common, fueled by the negative ego.

While the spiritual challenge we all face is over identification with our ego self, addicts experience this to an extreme. It's what I now refer to as *the disease* in my own recovery work. In its most destructive days, it was that voice that told me I didn't have a problem and that alcohol wasn't negatively impacting my life. Which led to years of great pain and what became a very secretive life, literally and figuratively. I took great strides to hide it from most people around me—friends, colleagues, and family—but also from *myself*. My mind told me I didn't have a problem despite many debilitating experiences, from blackouts to car accidents and behavior I wasn't proud of. Through this, my mind was all-powerful in maintaining this lie to *me*, despite the overwhelming evidence that suggested otherwise.

When I finally surrendered, it was through the experience of deep desperation that allowed for a "moment of clarity," where I was able to accept the truth that was always in my heart. I now understand that my heart *always* knew the truth, but because my mind dominated all, it took me many years to hear it.

So, why am I sharing this and how does it relate to my quest for soul purpose, and to this lesson in particular? It has been through my battle with addiction that I've learned what the ego self is capable of and just how powerful it can be, when we allow it. In fact, without a deep understanding of the ego through the lens of addiction, I wouldn't be doing the work I'm doing today.

The Career My Mind Wanted

Addiction was just one of the ways my mind led me astray from my truth. In my college days, my head led me to believe that my purpose was to work in advertising. I thought that I could be happy by doing something creative that was also a proven and accepted way to make money; it was a practical decision. Before I even got started on my journey, I had already censored my feelings.

The truth was something entirely different. Deep down, I wanted to act or create stories that awakened and inspired people. But I couldn't fathom myself as an actor, teacher, motivational speaker or filmmaker. My heart was telling me to pursue one thing, but my head was telling me to be *practical and reasonable*, which I defined as something that had a high chance for success. Something proven and safe. The advertising industry represented this for me, whereas a more artistic endeavor did not. Ultimately, my head won and continued to win for many, many years.

I came to know and begin to accept my soul purpose as a coach, mentor, and spiritual teacher, as I allowed my heart to lead the way. It's an ongoing process, even at the time of writing this book. But, the more I let go of who I *think* I am, instead embracing who my heart tells me I *really* am, the more relieved I feel. After a long and excruciating denial of my true desires, it feels like releasing my breath after holding it until I'm blue in the face. And even though I still don't understand *how* it's happening, I find peace in knowing that it *will* happen.

The Heart Truth

If you take one bit of advice away from this book, let it be this: *Your heart is where the truth lies.* The mind, or ego self, has good intentions, but it will not lead you to your soul purpose. The ego self's primary purpose is to protect you and preserve a version of yourself that it's taken great care to create. This version of you is not aligned to you living your soul purpose.

In fact, it subscribes to a false set of illusions that create a skewed version of the world you live in. The ego's goal is to keep these illusions intact, almost like a carefully constructed house of cards. When you perceive these illusions as real, true happiness almost surely evades you. In my instance, my life was the equivalent to an ongoing risk assessment; I was not allowing my feelings to lead the way. That's why the key to soul purpose is quieting the mind and putting a microphone to the heart.

For a long time, this was especially hard for me to come to terms with because I prided myself on being an intellectual. I had a full scholarship to Cornell University! Was I to let go of everything that got me to where I was and instead follow a whim? It took me a long time to surrender this part of myself, but when you become unhappy enough, surrender becomes easy.

What I've come to know is that "thinking with your heart" doesn't mean you have to throw intellect and rational thinking out the window. Far from it. Some of the greatest philosophies, discoveries, and inventions have come from great analytical minds. Enter: Albert Einstein and Stephen Hawking. A closer look at their work reveals how they allowed their intuition, or a deeper spiritual knowing, to lead their minds to unimaginable success.

Einstein famously said, "The intuitive mind is a sacred gift and the rational mind is a faithful servant. We have created a society that honors the servant and has forgotten the gift." Hawking once told the *New York Times Magazine*, "There is no prescribed route to follow to arrive at a new idea. You have to make the intuitive leap." In short, both men acknowledged that something higher may have been at play in their success.

Love Versus Fear

Another way to think about the heart versus the mind is to dig a level deeper. The heart-versus-mind war is best understood in terms of another war: love versus fear. Though it's important to note, the concept of "a war" is inherently an illusion. I only use the analogy to make a point. By their nature, being heart-led is synonymous with aligning to love, whereas when you lead with the mind, fear is your primary driver. Balance between the two is not the answer; the heart needs to have a higher proportion in the equation. When this happens, the fear completely subsides and the heart-led mind serves in the way it's supposed to, as a manifestation tool for the heart—not the commander.

Let's go back to my example. In college, my heart was telling me that my purpose was to awaken people through a creative endeavor. However, my mind jumped in and said things like this:

> *You can't make money being an artist!*
> *That sounds really difficult.*
> *That's not pragmatic at all.*
> *Do you want to spend your life suffering?*
> *One in a million succeed at that.*

I could go on and on listing the negative thoughts that my mind presented to me. The point is that all of these thoughts were *fear-based illusions*. They weren't actually true, but it felt like they were. Moreover, my heart-to-head ratio was way out of balance because my head won this argument at the time and took me far away from living my soul purpose. In short, because my fearful mind won, I compromised my true self for a very long time.

In fact, I ended up spending years allowing my head (fear) to lead the way. Until one day when I woke up and found myself deeply mentally, emotionally, and physically unwell. I had to get a place of intense despair to start listening to my heart. When I did, everything that was plaguing me began to slip away.

What I've come to learn is that your heart has all the answers you ever need. Therefore, to come to know your soul purpose requires you to listen to your heart. Really listen. What does it want? Namely, what do *you* really want? By accepting and surrendering to the answer, no matter how wild or impossible it seems, your calling will begin to reveal itself.

Only Your Heart Knows Your Soul Purpose

Why?

Hearing and accepting what your heart really wants is how you begin to understand your soul purpose. Think of your heart as a beautiful labyrinth, full of winding paths, but with only one path that leads to the center. In this practice, we locate that path—the pure awareness that exists in your heart's center. Only here will you find the answers you seek about your soul purpose.

For the purposes of this lesson, we're exploring your life's calling or "work." However, when you are living your soul purpose, it doesn't feel like work. It's important to note that as you first begin this work, you might be so exhausted from your current environment that all your heart wants is to go on vacation for a year. While that might be something you need at the moment, it's likely not what you want to do every day for the next ten years. Keep this idea in mind.

The Practice: Soul Listening

The purpose of *soul listening* is to hear what your true self already knows. Your heart is the communication gateway to your higher self. There are many soul listening practices, meditation being a key one. If you don't have a meditation practice, I highly recommend you adopt one, as that will help to accelerate this process. Additionally, understanding how to quiet the mind is essential to *living* your soul purpose, as you'll find in lessons ahead. However, for the purpose of this exercise, we're going to use a writing technique designed to reach the inner corners of your heart.

This practice should be done as many times as needed until you feel you've tapped into the core essence of your soul purpose. When you realize it, you'll know. More on this below.

What You'll Need

- A journal to write in. Feel free to use the same journal for all your soul purpose lessons. As indicated earlier, I suggest dating your work, so you can reflect back on your progress at some point.
- A pen or pencil.
- A quiet place that enables you to be fully present.

How to Do It

Sitting in a quiet place, without distraction, follow these simple steps:

Step 1: Conduct a simple invocation to invite your true self in to help you with this exercise. Do so by closing your eyes, taking a few deep breaths to center and ground, and then recite the following aloud:

I invite in the highest divine guidance of love and light and my higher self to be with me now. Please help me come to know my soul calling by opening my heart and quieting my mind in this exercise. Please guide me completely. Show me how to take what I love, the unique gifts that have been bestowed upon me, and how I can best serve—to reveal my truth. According to divine will and for the highest light and love of all. And so it is!

Step 2: Get ready to practice a *free-writing exercise* that taps into the truth of your higher self. Here's how:

- After your invocation in Step 1, consciously clear your

mind by spending about a minute imagining a white light entering in the top of your head and wiping it of all negative thoughts. Imagine this light as a beautiful waterfall, clearing and cleansing all forms of fear and doubt away.

- o You can also close your eyes and picture staring at a blank white screen for the same amount of time. Imagine as you stare at this image that all forms of negativity are leaving your mind.

- Next, imagine you are literally dropping into your heart, which opens like a beautiful flower. It is from here that you will write.
- Then, open your eyes and answer one question at a time by simply allowing your thoughts to flow onto the page. Don't think, judge, or censor; just write.
- Don't worry about structure, grammar, or even making sense. If it's just random words that come out, great.
- Write until there is nothing you have left to say in response to each question in Step 3.

Step 3: Using the guidelines in the prior step, free-write a response to each of the questions below. Before each question, close your eyes and silently ask your heart to guide each question. You can re-center using the above steps at any time you feel your mind has taken over.

- What do I really want to do more than anything in the world?
- If I could spend my days doing _________, then I would be fulfilled.
- If money were no object, I'd spend my life doing_________.
- The thing I'm most passionate about doing is_____________.
- I've always dreamed about doing_________ for work.
- I know deep down that my true soul purpose is_______.

Your responses to each of these questions are clues, perhaps answers. In that respect, just observe what you write, don't assess it.

Step 4: Review your writing and make a list of any reoccurring themes or potential soul calling endeavors that speak to you. Here's what your list might look like:

- World traveler
- Actress
- Animal rescuer
- Yoga teacher
- Business owner

Step 5: Categorize your responses using the chart below. You'll want to toss out responses that are merely a *reaction to your current environment*. For example, if you're currently overworked, you might think you'd like to sit on your couch the rest of your life and eat pizza. But do you really? Likewise, people often have travel as a desire, but is traveling what you want to spend all your time doing? If so, then this might be core to your soul purpose.

Next, do your best to identify which are hobbies versus life callings. A life calling is something you can imagine spending nearly all your time doing. It fills your heart completely, whereas a hobby is a part-time interest. Again, allow your heart to guide your work here. If you find your mind taking over, repeat Steps 1 and 2.

Possibility Categorization

Possible soul purpose	Do I really want to spend 50%+ of my time doing this?	Is this a hobby or a life calling?
World Traveler	No	Hobby
Actress	Yes	Hobby
Animal rescuer	No	Hobby
Yoga teacher	Yes	Life Calling
Business owner	Yes	Life Calling

Step 6: Allow your heart to guide you in a *heart meter* rating. You can write this down if you choose, but it's not necessary. Be sure to consciously drop into your heart and ask it to guide your response here. Know that if something sets your heart on fire, you'll feel deep excitement and resonance about it. Physically, you might feel tingly or your heart might flutter. It might also feel scary, but in a good, exciting way.

Possible soul purpose	Sets heart on fire (1-10)
Yoga teacher	Sets my heart on blazing fire - 10!
Business owner	It lights me up – 7

Step 7: If you nailed it in your first try, fantastic. How will you know? By being honest with yourself. If you have a sense that there's more to the story, repeat it again a week later, and again, until you know your truth. Additionally, as you practice some of the later lessons tied to fear and limiting beliefs, come back to this exercise and revisit it to see if you uncover a new, different truth.

Step 8: You will be certain that you've realized your soul purpose because nothing will feel more right. You will have the sense you are coming home. Here are some questions you can use to guide you.

- Is this something you've always secretly wanted to do but perhaps were afraid to voice it to others?
- When you imagine doing this thing and being successful at it, does it bring you absolute joy?
- Does it both excite you and scare you?
- When you imagine not doing this, do you feel a sense of loss or deep disappointment?
- Is there anything you can imagine doing instead of this that would bring you even greater happiness?
- Have you deep down, on some level, always known that this is what you were meant to do?

Remember, this lesson is about the journey; one that has no right or wrong answers to it. It's an ever-evolving experience. Whenever you feel that you are trying to figure something out, you are off track. Whatever your heart is telling you in this moment, trust it and move on. And trust that in doing so, the answers you seek will be revealed when you are ready to receive them.

CHAPTER 3

Ask for What You Want

"Don't look for your dreams to become true;
look to become true to your dreams."
- Michael Beckwith

Once you have come to know your soul purpose, you have to ask for it. When we ask the universe for what we want, we open ourselves up to receiving it. For those of us who have a hard time asking for help, like me, this will be particularly powerful. By simply taking the action of asking, we open ourselves up to the gift of receiving from and co-creating with the divine—the life force energy that surrounds us all. This energy is also called *God, Source, a higher power,* or simply the universal energy of love; feel free to use any concept that aligns with your beliefs.

Asking is also a powerful means of both affirming and surrendering to what you want. Your dreams are no longer denied or hidden. When you ask the universe for what you want, it's another way of saying, "Hey universe, I'm ready to do this and to commit myself fully to this!" You are showing the universe that you believe your dream is possible, and that you are ready to become true to them. You are ready to step in, fully and completely.

If, like me, you have spent the vast majority of your life, denying your soul purpose, when you take the action of asking the universe for what you want, a sense of freedom often comes about. For me, this freedom was synonymous with an uninhibited feeling of hope. It was like chains that had been holding me down suddenly unshackled.

My Corporate Life

I mentioned earlier that I first began to initiate the compromise of my true self in college. Plagued by fear and a number of beliefs which didn't serve my highest good, I decided to study advertising, as a "smart" and "safe" choice. While I have nothing against advertising, this just wasn't what I *really* wanted to do.

Deep down, I wanted to study theater, writing, film, or English literature—something artistic and tied to the humanities. But I believed this wasn't a viable path and would only lead to a life of struggle. By choosing advertising, I rationalized, I could be in a creative field but also have the opportunity to make it the *real world*, whereas a life in an artistic endeavor would only be marked by hardship and failure. These were the thoughts that frequented my mind.

I willingly shed my true desires and received a Bachelor's and Master's degree in my chosen respective fields. When I was finished with college, I landed a job at a big advertising agency in San Francisco. Pushing aside my prior true desires, I came to believe that this job was going to be everything I wanted.

About two months into the job, I started having debilitating panic attacks. Attacks that came about as an absolute onslaught of terror, where I was mentally and physically paralyzed and had a hard time functioning. I'd have them periodically in meetings and eventually began having them every single day, while on public transportation, on my way to work. They became constant and ruthless.

It was one of the most frightening and darkest times of my life. I'd have to leave the office to catch my breath, get off the train at an unplanned stop—the disruption to basic life tasks seemed to only be accelerating. On one occasion, I ended up in the emergency room. After spending the day in the hospital, I'll never forget what one of the doctors said to me after spending time talking to me and assessing my situation. "I think you're having these panic attacks because you are so depressed that your body doesn't know what to do." That was a moment I'll never forget. It was the hard truth that I hadn't encountered until that instant.

Following this, I began to self-medicate in ways I hadn't before. No longer just reserved for weekends, I began to feel the need to drink excessively during the week, merely to get through it. And the weekends became increasingly reckless; I was staying out to all hours of the night trying to escape into oblivion. It began to feel like a destructive need that I couldn't satisfy, a way to cope and survive, and in essence, a bottomless pit. While being unhappy in my life didn't cause my addiction, it did serve to exacerbate it.

The truth was that I hated my job and the life I was living. Every time I tried to imagine spending more than eight hours a day for the rest of my life doing it, I would panic. It felt like a life sentence. I remember thinking that I couldn't believe that this was all there was—that human existence, my existence—was to work every day in a job I didn't like and then die. Is this what I had worked so hard in school for? This? The thoughts that played on repeat in my mind at that time were things like:

> *This is it? This is what I spent all that time studying for?*
> *How am I going to do this for 40+ years?*
> *Is this being adult? Work in a job you hate, and then you die?!*
> *This can't be my entire existence; it just can't be.*

I realize now that my soul was literally screaming out to me. I was in shock. I thought, *am I just naïve? Am I selfish because I want more for my life?* I decided I wasn't any of these things. In part, my higher self decided it for me, because the panic attacks didn't subside and trying to manage them became unbearable. So I quit.

I decided to listen to where my heart was calling me to, and that was to Los Angeles to pursue acting.

Guess what? Once I made this move, the attacks stopped completely. I'd love to say that from here I stepped fully into living with purpose each day and never took another job again that didn't provide soul-level fulfillment, but it's never that easy. After a couple of years pursuing acting, I wound up back at another big corporate job. Still ruled by fear, I didn't know how to stay committed to my dreams.

But I learned a few things during that time. I learned that your heart is always speaking to you, whether or not you choose to listen to it. I also learned that nothing feels as good as leaping, taking a risk, and pursuing a dream. But I also learned that the path to soul purpose requires patience and trust, which I greatly lacked at the time. In short, I wasn't ready. I had a lot more to learn.

To New York City

My renewed corporate career took me from Los Angeles to New York City in 2007, where I would end up spending another several years trying to climb the corporate ladder. I'd become resigned. So, working in environments that didn't feed my soul, just my wallet, became my reality. I'd accepted that this is what grown-ups do.

And while I was miserable and tired, from the long hours to the toxic politics, the panic attacks didn't resurface because I had switched something off. In part, I had again turned to alcohol to numb myself and escape an unhappy existence following a brief period of sobriety. As a result, I had shut off a big part of my heart, and with that, hope. But anyone who's tried to block such an important part of yourself will tell you that it only lasts for so long, because the universe always has other plans.

At this point in my journey, the world I was living in was

happening *to me*, not *for me*. Living in this mindset, I spent the next four years in jobs I dreaded every single day, often working for 80 hours a week or longer. In one job, I was at the office so much that I ate the majority of my meals there, gaining a considerable amount of weight. Often, the cleaning staff would come in at night and leave, and I'd still be there. Beyond the long hours, the work itself held no meaning for me. And the office gossip and people who didn't treat me or one other well only made it worse. I was spending nearly all of my waking hours doing something I hated because I didn't believe I had a choice.

When you're working this much doing something you don't love, it's also hard to spend any time practicing self-care or attending to your own wellbeing. This was definitely the case for me. I was drinking a bottle of wine every night that I wasn't at work, as a way to alleviate my suffering, which only worsened my overall wellbeing. As a result, the world was once again a dark place for me. And I didn't realize then that it was entirely of my own making. I was no victim, even though I felt like one.

But I still had an ounce of hope. It was small, but present. I've come to know that sometimes, we have to go deep into the darkness to learn the lesson we need to learn. This was definitely the case for me. Because I took that hope and I began to ask for something I wanted. A way out.

The way out of this situation that I dreamed for myself was that I would be laid off and receive a big severance which would allow me to travel. I started imagining it and praying for it. At first, it was a means of escape, to think about the possibility. Then, it slowly became something I started to cautiously believe in. Then it became almost a *waking mantra*, as real as anything—a reality that would indeed happen. This is what hope can offer in our moments of despair. I took this one kernel of hope and I asked the universe clearly for what I wanted, with conviction, and often.

Then, to my surprise, it happened.

Ask the Universe for What You Want

Why?

What I've learned is that once we know what we want, we must ask for it. In this moment of asking we acknowledge our joint partnership with the divine and open the channels to receive. We gently step out of the idea that we are a victim of the world and instead affirm our part in the creation of our own circumstances. When we initially ask for what we want, as in this practice, it's like an invocation. You are sparking a new timeline filled with higher possibilities for your life.

The Practice: Intentional Asking

When you intentionally ask for something, you invoke it into being. It's important that you don't beg, plead, or wish for it. You ask with the mindset that you deserve what you want through affirming your request from a place of authentic belief and power. The initial request only needs to happen once, as long as you continue to affirm what you want through your actions. Then, continually ask for help each step of the way and you shall receive, which we'll practice more in Lesson 8.

What You'll Need

- A quiet place that enables you to be fully present

How to Do It

Sitting in a quiet place, without distraction, follow these simple steps:

Step 1: First, be clear on what you're going to ask with respect to your soul purpose. For example, if you have become certain that your soul purpose is to be a yoga teacher, then get ready to ask the universe to help you make it possible.

Step 2: Once you are clear on the ask, close your eyes and take a few deep breaths to ground and center yourself.

Step 3: Ask divine love and your higher self to be present with you.

Step 4: With your eyes still closed, imagine a that there is beautiful white light all around you. Feel this light and breathe it in, slowly and deeply. Then, ask for the assistance of this light to open your heart and quiet your mind. You can imagine this light wiping away all current thoughts out of your mind like wiping a clean slate, while your heart opens as if it were a beautiful lotus flower.

Step 5: Imagine in front of you a beautiful angel or guide of the highest light and love. Whatever image works best for you. If you're religious, it may be tied to your specific beliefs. Imagine that this guide is your soul purpose guide and that they are here to help you manifest your life calling.

Step 6: Keeping your eyes closed, place your hand over your heart and ask for what you want. When you ask, affirm what you believe and know in your heart already, while asking for assistance in making it possible. Ask from a place of positivity. You should feel confident, blissful, and excited. Here is an example of how to intentionally ask.

Intentional Asking Example

I believe my purpose is to be a yoga teacher. I feel this in my heart and in every part of my entire being. I can see it, feel it, touch it and when I do, I feel a bliss and sense of peace that I've never known before. It is my truth. Which is why I hereby affirm that this is my life calling and further affirm that I am open to receiving this gift. I ask for the entire lighted universe to help me in realizing my dream. Show me what to do, one step at a time. According to divine will for the highest good of all. And so it is!

Step 7: Feel free to do this a few times until you really feel you've asked and been heard. You'll know this based on how free and at peace you feel with regard to whether or not it's happening. If fear is creeping in, push it aside and reaffirm your request.

Use intentional asking every day and for guidance at every step in your soul purpose journey. We'll spend more time on this in Lesson 8.

CHAPTER 4

The Human Experience of Fear

"The fears you don't face control you.
The fears you face, you move beyond."
- Wayne Dyer

The antithesis of living in soul purpose, a heart-centered endeavor, is to live in fear. As I said earlier, it's how I spent a great majority of my adult life. But I'm not alone in this. In fact, the lesson we all come here to learn, at some level, is to rise above fear and choose love as our dominant everyday, every-moment experience. This includes allowing love to fuel our thoughts, choices, and actions instead of letting worry, doubt, dread—the many forms of fear—take over.

To align with our true self, instead of our ego self is the objective. Think of the ego as a construct we have created to help us survive in a difficult world. The ego views the world as a scary place and considers its chief job to navigate it. You'll always know the ego because it speaks to you from a place of fear, whereas the higher self speaks from the perspective of love. Ego says, "You're not good enough, smart enough, or strong enough." The higher self says, "You are loved and perfect just as you are." The good news is that since we created it, we can also direct it, with practice, which we'll learn more about later on.

For now, just know that when it comes to living your soul purpose, every day will become a lesson in choosing love (higher self) over fear (ego self). Soul purpose is in fact how you align deeper with your true self. Why? Because our ego wants us to repress, bury, and ignore our true calling. Everyone's true calling is anchored in some form of love and the ego doesn't know or understand love.

How Fear Blocks Our Dreams

When I was a kid, I had big dreams, long before I went to college and started denying them (or later, when I started drinking to muffle them). Like most children, I was full of hope. I lived in a world where anything was possible. My aspirations knew no limits. I was going to be in the movies, as an actress, director, and writer. Or, I was going to be a motivational speaker. Either way, I was going to travel and see the world. I was going to be someone who inspired people on a mass scale. Nothing seemed too big or overwhelming to achieve. I whole-heartedly believed in my dreams.

Then, as adulthood set in, these dreams began to subside. Sound familiar?

That's because nearly all of us go through it. It is *the* lesson we have engrained in us. We all are here to learn how to align with the divine or love. I, myself, had to learn how to walk through the fear that taught me to deprive myself by denying my inner calling. I had to learn how to take action in spite of my fears. The universe, as it does, presented several tests along the way.

One of the first tests I received was at around age 12. I faced a huge disappointment when I didn't get a role in a play that I wanted. I was devastated. Quickly, another series of disappointments followed. It was then that I began to adopt a series of fear-based beliefs that carried me into adulthood. Things like:

> *Money, success, bliss—they're not for everybody.*
> *I'm not talented enough, smart enough, or pretty enough.*
> *I can't do what I love and make money...That's not realistic.*
> *Bad things happen to good people.*
> *No pain, no gain.*

It was during this time that I first learned to abandon hope that my dreams were possible. As I got older, I became completely indoctrinated with these illusions, which ultimately led me to the misery I described.

Can you relate to any of this? Most of us end up becoming ruled by a thousand forms of fear, trapped in our self-created prison. We forget who we really are and disconnect from the part of ourselves that knows the truth as love.

Stepping into your soul purpose will require you to reject the illusion of fear and align to love. As Marianne Williamson put it in her best-selling book, *Return to Love*[4], "Our deepest fear is not that we are inadequate. Our deepest fear is that we are powerful beyond measure. It is our light, not our darkness that most frightens us." To initiate this path, first identifying the fears that are entrapping you, and even enslaving you is crucial. Only when you surrender to the fears that are dictating your life, can you step into living your dreams.

How Fear Manifests as Addiction

As I talked about earlier, one of the great energies of addiction is the ego, or fear. As such, recovery is often a spiritual process; at least it has been for me. In recovery, you learn how to surrender your fears, from surrendering to the addiction itself to learning how to continuously choose love over fear each day through staying sober.

In fact, I have realized through my recovery that what manifested in me as addiction was largely *an inability to cope with fear*. This isn't to say that I didn't inherit "the gene" or have a serious physical and mental disease; I did and do. But it's the understanding of the spiritual nature of this disease that has been essential to my understanding of fear.

---

[4]Marianne Williamson, Return to Love, 1992.

In short, I had a million fears but they all really boiled down to one: *I felt separate and alone.* The answer to this and to my recovery has been an alignment to the one truth, which is love. In fact, I've come to understand that no matter what the problem, my answer is always a realignment to the universal consciousness of love, which is at the center of all things. An understanding that's been deepened through my study of *A Course in Miracles*,[5] a divinely channeled book in which a miracle is defined as *a shift in perception from fear to love.*

However, it has been and continues to be a process. But I know that through a continual surrender to the fears that plague me most, do I more deeply align with my soul purpose. This is because soul purpose is about the path of the heart.

The Fear that Plagues Us Most

One of the greatest fear-based illusions to which we all subscribe is the fear of death, or separation. This fear manifests in many forms and is likely the root of the majority of your fears. In fact, most of us spend the majority of our lives feeling separate and disconnected from our fellow human beings because we don't view ourselves as *one* with *divine source* or God. Our fear of death only serves to heighten this, as we view it as a form of permanent separation. You'll see when you begin to identify your deepest fears that they're all tied to separation or death in some form. Therefore, the most important work you can do toward becoming free from your fears will be to surrender your fear of death and the illusions around separation to which they are tied.

As we'll explore in this lesson, you'll need to reevaluate your beliefs about death as a form of separation and finality. For example, is death an absolute end or is it a beautiful transition?

---

[5] Foundation for Inner Peace, A Course in Miracles, 1975.

When people we love die, are they really gone or are they closer than ever? Are we ever separate from the divine presence that many of us know as God? These are the types of beliefs you'll need to reconsider as you embark on surrendering to all of your fears so you may fully step into your life calling.

____

Surrender Your Deepest Fears

Why?

If you're ruled by your fears, living your soul purpose is nearly impossible. That's why regular surrender to your fears is some of the most important work you can do. At first, you will need to practice conscious surrender. Meaning, that you may still feel the fear, but are choosing to not be ruled by it. You'll practice taking actions in spite of your fears. In time and with enough practice, the fears will subside, and the conscious effort won't be required.

The Practice: What-if Fear Game

The _what if fear-game_ is some of the most powerful work you can do on a regular basis to surrender to your fears. Use this practice anytime fear has become an obstacle to living your soul purpose, or when you are making an important decision. The goal of this exercise is to surrender to the fear that's blocking you, knowing that even if the worst thing you can imagine does indeed happen, you will be OK.

What You'll Need

- A journal to write in. As indicated before, feel free to use the same journal for all your soul purpose lessons.
- A pen or pencil.
- A quiet place that enables you to be fully present.

How to Do It

Sitting in a quiet place, without distraction, follow these simple steps:

Step 1: Take a few deep breaths to ground and center yourself. Quietly ask for divine guidance and your higher self to step in and assist you in releasing the fears that are blocking you from your purpose.

Step 2: Identify the decision or obstacle that's causing you to experience fear. Here are some examples:

- I'm afraid to quit my job and start a business.
- I'm afraid to leave my job to be with my kids.
- I'm afraid to take time to travel.
- I'm afraid to switch careers.
- I'm afraid to go back to school.
- I'm afraid of not being able to pay my bills this month.
- I'm afraid of getting sick.

Step 3: Write down the thing you are afraid of at the top of a clean piece of paper in your journal.

Step 4: Under the fear at the top of the page, write the phrase "what if" under it five times.

I'm afraid to quit my job and start my own business.
What if
What if
What if
What if
What if

Step 5: List all the potential things you are most afraid of happening from following this potential course of action or fear obstacle. Make sure the fears are different from one another. If you can't fill all five spots, that's okay.

I'm afraid to quit my job and start my own business.
What if I fail
What if I lose my retirement
What if I can't put food on the table
What if I'm laughed at
What if it's harder than I realize

Step 6: Now, take each "what if" scenario and play it out until you've reached the thing you are the most afraid of happening. Make sure you push the fear as deep as you can go, by using "if I x, then x" as outlined below to get to the root cause. Identify your core fear at the end.

Example 1

I'm afraid to quit my job and start my own business.
What if I fail?
If I fail, then I could lose all my money
If I lose all my money, then I could be homeless
If I'm homeless, I'll be hungry and could get sick
If I'm hungry and sick, I could die
My core fear is death

Example 2

I'm afraid to quit my job and start my own business.
What if it's harder than I realize?
If it's harder than I realize, I won't succeed
If I don't succeed, I'll have to find a job again
If I have to find a job again, it could be worse than the one I have now
If it's worse than the one I have now, I'll slip into clinical depression
If slip into clinical depression, I won't be able to work
If I can't work, I won't be able to take care of my family
If I can't take care of my family, I'll have to ask my parents for help
If I have to ask my parents for help, I'll lose all my self-worth and dignity
If I lose all my self-worth and dignity, I don't think I'll ever be whole again
My core fear is losing myself and never being whole again

Step 7: Now, make a *decision* to surrender to the core fear.

Surrender is a decision that you make, particularly in the beginning of your practice. It's aided by re-evaluating the thoughts and belief systems you have tied to this fear, which we'll explore more in the next lesson.

Use this process to surrender your fears:

Example 1: Fear of Death

1.	*Say aloud: I hereby surrender to my core fear of death and the power it holds over my actions and life choices.*
2.	**List the beliefs that fuel your fear:** End of existence, separation from loved ones, painful, only live once.
3.	**Create new beliefs:**
	I choose to believe that death is not an end, but a beginning.
	I choose to believe that death is a transition to something greater.
	I choose to believe that death brings us closer to our loved ones, not further away.
4.	**Affirm these beliefs by saying them aloud.**

Really feel into the truth of your new beliefs, while reflecting upon how the beliefs that have fueled your fear have kept you from pursuing what you want in life. Consciously affirm to no longer let these fears control your life.

Step 8: Continue your practice of surrendering your core fears. This should be both a conscious and a spiritual endeavor. True spiritual surrender can happen in an instant or over time. The above steps are mostly the conscious part of the process. To deepen the spiritual experience, use the practice of intentional asking to initiate the release of them from the other parts of you, like the subconscious mind. Below is an example of an affirmative prayer you can use:

I call on the divine and my higher self to assist me in completely and permanently releasing all the fears that currently reside in my conscious and subconscious fields–including my emotional, mental, physical, etheric, and spiritual bodies. I ask that any fears that are blocking me from living my highest possible purpose on this planet be released now. I affirm that I am ready to completely let go of any power they hold over me now. I affirm the only truth there is, divine love. And so it is!

Know that releasing your fears is a lifelong process. It's the lesson we have come here to master. However, every time you participate in this practice, you will experience a shift. And every shift has a deeply profound experience on your reality. There are no small shifts when it comes to the release of fear. All are transformative.

CHAPTER 5

The Reality of Illusions

"You have the ability to quickly change your patterns of thought, and eventually your life experience."
- Abraham Hicks

Our thoughts and beliefs create our reality—good and bad. As I discussed earlier, I spent most of my adult life driven by a false set of limiting beliefs anchored in the illusion of fear and separation. But to me, they were very real, and my reality reflected as much. This leads me to the essence of our next lesson: Many of the beliefs you currently have are in fact illusions, created *by* and *for* the ego.

Limiting Belief Systems

Limiting beliefs are illusions that serve to keep us constrained in some way. For example, one of the ones most often subscribed to—scarcity—keeps us in a never-ending cycle of just trying to survive. When we live in survival consciousness, every day is a struggle to make it to the next. In this state of existence, our primary focus is on things like having a roof over our head, paying our monthly bills, or putting food on the table. Of course, this is indeed the reality for many people on the planet. But for a lot of people, it's a result of a collective belief in scarcity. For others, it's more specifically self-induced.

Self-inflicted survival consciousness happens when we adapt a series of beliefs, often untrue, about what we need to survive.

Having these things becomes as real as your need for food or water. You create a desired reality that is necessary to your existence, and keeps you in a perpetual mode of just hanging on. For example, you might believe that living in a certain neighborhood, having a certain car, house, lifestyle, or schools for your children are essential to your survival. They feel critical to your very existence. The thought of not having them or losing them can feel the equivalent to death or loss. Is this something you can resonate with?

Victimhood is another limiting belief system that most humans have subscribed to at some point in their life. In this state of being, we believe the world is happening *to* us, not *for* us. Largely driven by the idea that destiny is something that's fixed, we view ourselves as powerless in creating and shaping our life. Our days are an endless cycle of feeling that we are a victim to our circumstance, helpless to effect any real change. Common thoughts tied to this state of being include:

Why does this always happen to me?
I have such bad luck.
The universe hates me.

In victim consciousness, you are oblivious to the role you play in your own life experiences. You are ignorant to the ways in which you are *co-creating your life*. Every thought, emotion and action directly creates the reality you experience, which we'll practice more of in Lesson 7.

The Subconscious Mind

As you work on understanding the fear-based illusions and their corresponding limiting belief systems that shape your reality, it's important to understand a bit about the subconscious mind. Think of the subconscious mind as a big storage warehouse that files away your beliefs, memories, and life experiences. This information plays an important role in creating the reality you live in, including how you perceive events, and therefore the way you respond to certain situations emotionally or behaviorally. Both are influenced by what's stored there.

For example, if you struggle with money and financial abundance, you likely have certain beliefs about money that are influencing your situation. Perhaps you think that money is hard to come by, or even more deeply, that you don't deserve the rewards money provides. Both of these beliefs serve to shape your experience with money, or lack thereof. You may notice that when you're having a conversation about money, you feel anxious or fearful. This is because your subconscious mind has stored false beliefs about money, causing you to think you're in danger when you're not. A strong indicator that your beliefs about money require examination.

As we dive into our work in this lesson, it's important to understand how your perception is influenced by your subconscious programming. Particularly because your subconscious mind adheres to "you get what you focus on." So, start considering how your life experiences and the corresponding beliefs you've formed or have been taught have influenced what's stored in your subconscious.

My Inner Victim and Survivor

Earlier, I described about how I spent the majority of my adult life working in jobs I hated, for anywhere from 60–80+ hours a week, miserable, and deeply unhappy. During this time, I was living in both a state of survival and a victim consciousness, which later became heightened by my addiction to alcohol.

As part of this, I had come to believe that I needed a high-paying job no matter what the cost to me, my health, or my wellbeing. That without this salary and the status quo that had become my life, I would be lost. I also believed that I had little power to change my circumstance. That this was in some way my destiny and there was nothing much I could do about it. Through adopting these belief systems, I was imprisoning myself in a never-ending cycle of fear. Until I put an end to it.

Here's why this matters. Without shedding the limiting beliefs that fueled my survival consciousness, I would never have been able to step into my soul purpose. Limiting beliefs are the blockers to soul purpose. They are fear-based patterns of thought that muffle the voice of your heart.

If you resonate with this, you are not alone. Nearly everyone on the planet experiences the reality of living with limiting beliefs. However, if they're ruling your daily life, you likely feel trapped, like you're on a hamster wheel you can't get off. Unfortunately, soul purpose doesn't exist here. Only fear does.

However, when you see your limiting beliefs for what they are—illusions—reality as you know it will start to change. That's why soul purpose work requires us to release the limiting beliefs that bind us. When we do, we make room for thoughts and beliefs that are supportive of our dreams.

Release the Limiting Beliefs That Bind You

Why?

Fear-based illusions and negative thought patterns, such as limiting beliefs, are what keep us from living our dreams. You've already done work to release some of your fears around soul purpose. However, the deeper construct of the limiting beliefs that shape these fears also need to be addressed to prevent the same cycle of fear from playing on continual repeat. That's why in this practice, we take a look at the major and minor belief systems that comprise your current reality.

The Practice: Limiting Belief Release

The practice of *releasing your limiting beliefs* is one that will likely be a long process. It's taken you a long time to construct these beliefs; don't expect removing them to happen overnight. The practice involves both written and meditative work to release the beliefs from your conscious and subconscious mind. In particular, we'll use a practice for the subconscious mind that is almost like a form of hypnosis. However, there are many others to consider as well, including reiki and other forms of energy healing, as well as, emotional freedom techniques (EFT)[6].

While this practice can be used for any situation or goal, we'll focus on the limiting beliefs that are potentially blocking you from living your purpose. It's a good idea to use this practice every few weeks to start.

---

[6] https://en.wikipedia.org/wiki/Emotional_Freedom_Techniques

What You'll Need

- A journal to write in
- A pen or pencil
- A quiet place that enables you to be fully present

How to Do It

Sitting in a quiet place, without distraction, follow these simple steps:

Step 1: As always, take a few deep breaths to center and ground yourself in the moment.

Step 2: Call in your higher self and divine guidance to assist you in this exercise. You can imagine a beautiful white light around you as you say this:

I call forth divine guidance and my higher self to assist me in releasing the limiting beliefs that no longer serve me. Specifically those that are blocking me from living my soul purpose. According to divine will and for the highest good of all. And so it is!

Step 3: Now, quietly ask your higher self to show you the beliefs that are blocking you from living your soul purpose, before you begin writing.

Step 4: Write down <u>all</u> the limiting beliefs that come to you. Again, a limiting belief is any fear-based illusion that restrains us in some way. Feel free to use the list below as guidance.

Examples of Limiting Beliefs		
I'm too old or young	Soul purpose and money are separate	The world is happening to me
Happiness is a destination	I don't deserve to be happy	Work is just a reality of life
Love has to be earned	Dreams aren't real	I'm not creative enough
Change is hard	Not everyone can be Oprah	It's too late to change

Work is hard	I'm destined to be poor	I have no clue who I am
Life is hard	I'm powerless	I could never do that
Money is hard to come by	I'm not self-disciplined enough	My family will abandon me
Not everyone can be rich	A 9-5 job is the only way to make money	I don't have the support to try
Not everyone can be successful	If I quit my job, I'll hurt my chances	It's not possible to love your job
My plate is too full	I just have bad luck	No one will understand
I don't have enough time	There's no point in dreaming big	Love doesn't come easy
Money is the root of all evil	Not trying is better than failing	Being rich isn't spiritual
I'll never experience abundance	My health is holding me back	Spiritual work doesn't = money
I'm not smart enough	I'm not ready	I can't do it

Step 5: Next, make four columns in your journal. In the left column write the limiting beliefs that you identify with *the most*.

Limiting Beliefs			
I'm not smart enough			
Life is hard			
Dreams aren't real			
There isn't enough			

Step 6: Next, identify the root cause of each of your beliefs. Is it based on an experience you had? Something you were taught or have witnessed? Try to understand why you hold this belief. Again, ask for guidance when you feel stuck.

Limiting Beliefs	Root Cause		
I'm not smart enough	I always did poorly in school		
Life is hard	It's my experience		
Dreams aren't real	That's what I've learned		
There isn't enough	I've always been taught this		

Step 7: Now, explore what would happen if these beliefs weren't

true by answering the question, "What if this belief wasn't true?" If these beliefs weren't true, then what would be possible?

Limiting Beliefs	Root Cause	What If This Wasn't True	
I'm not smart enough	I always did poorly in school	I could be confident	
Life is hard	It's my experience	Each day would be blissful	
Dreams aren't real	That's what I've learned	I could do anything I want	
There isn't enough	I've always been taught this	I could be rich	

Step 8: Finally, consciously choose a new, empowering belief. Be sure your new belief is positive and uplifting and doesn't reinforce a negative. For example, "Life is not hard" versus "My life overflows with ease and bliss."

Limiting Beliefs	Root Cause	What If This Wasn't True	New Belief
I'm not smart enough	I always did poorly in school	I could be confident	I exude confidence and wisdom
Life is hard	It's my experience	Each day would be blissful	My life overflows with ease and bliss
Dreams aren't real	That's what I've learned	I could do anything I want	Every day is filled with endless possibilities
There isn't enough	I've always been taught this	I could be rich	The universe is overflowing with abundance

Step 9: Recite these new beliefs as affirmations aloud. Repeat them daily for as long as your inner guidance tells you is needed.

Step 10: Now, focus on releasing these beliefs from the subconscious mind. To do so, place your hands over your heart and ask for your higher self to be present and assist you in this process.

Step 11: Next, slowly repeat the script below. Take your time and pause where needed. *Do not rush through this.* Repeat this script for one belief at a time over the weeks ahead and at your own pace:

Even though I have believed (state the limiting belief), it no longer serves me. Therefore, I hereby ask for it to be removed now, fully, completely, and permanently, from my subconscious mind. As such, I direct my subconscious to remove this belief from every single aspect of my being—my physical, mental, emotional, and spiritual bodies, across all lines of time. I also hereby release all conscious and subconscious causes and reasons for having this belief. As I do any other thought patterns or belief systems that are tied to it. While I thank my ego for protecting me with this belief to this point in my life, I affirm it no longer has any power over me. It is finished. I am completely free to let it go. With the release of this belief, I am now free to (state the new belief). I affirm that this part of myself is now healed. And so it is!

Repeat the steps in this lesson as many times as needed. Here are some indicators you can use to assess when your practice for a specific belief is complete:

- You see clearly through the illusion of the belief; it no longer feels real.
- When you think about the belief, it no longer provokes a sense of fear.
- Your inner guidance tells you that you've let it go.

CHAPTER 6

Believe Your Dream is Possible

"If you give up on your dreams, what's left?"
- Jim Carrey

So far, you've learned how to get clear on what your heart wants, ask for what you want, and release the limiting beliefs that are blocking you from living your soul purpose. The next lesson that's critical to your soul purpose journey is *believing in your dream.* It's one thing to let go of beliefs that no longer serve us and another to practice continuous belief in the feasibility of your dream. However, both are innately intertwined.

It took me a long time to learn that if my heart can imagine it, it is possible. I didn't understand that my higher, all knowing self, speaks to me through my heart. And that my higher self holds the truth of what's possible for me on this planet. In other words, what my heart wants for me is actually what my higher self knows to be true. The great potential for our lives resides in our hearts, as our most precious dreams. We tackled some of this work in Lesson 2, as it's crucial to first get clear on what your dream is.

Next, comes the work of practicing continuous belief that what you want is indeed possible. Personally, I had to change the perspective I had about my dreams. For a long time, I viewed them as a source of torture, showing me what I desired but couldn't have. I also viewed them as nothing more than a means to escape my currently reality, fantasizing to get relief from an unhappy existence. Again, attaching the energy of *not possible* to my dreams.

It was only after a profound experience, when I decided to follow a seemingly wild dream, that I realized my desires were in fact clues to my soul purpose. Doing what my heart wanted me to do, despite how outrageous it seemed, is when I first began to step into a different life—one fueled by purpose.

My Journey Abroad

At the end of 2010, at 35 years old, I was working in an incredibly arduous corporate job that I didn't like, let alone love. I had become deeply unhappy. Little did I know that I was near the end of this particular life experience and would never repeat it again.

As I said, what I really wanted more than anything at the time was to be laid off, receive a healthy severance, and use it to travel. After I decided to ask the universe for this, I started praying it would happen. Then, I started believing it was possible. I could see it and feel it perfectly. I knew exactly where I was going to go, what I was going to do there and how it would feel. The vision of it was incredibly real, defined with detail.

Then, it happened. In December of 2010, I was laid off and received a healthier severance than I had even envisioned. Three weeks later, I had purchased a one-way ticket to Vietnam and subleased my apartment. By March, after wrapping up all of my responsibilities at work, I was gone.

This experience has become a defining moment in my life. It's when I learned that belief is core to the manifestation of your dreams, no matter how wild or outrageous they are. Even when everyone around me told me I was crazy to leave and travel instead of looking for another job, my belief persevered. The guidance of my heart could not be deterred. I had rarely felt so driven to do something.

Did any of it sound like the smart thing to do on paper? Absolutely not. But a gut feeling deep inside told me I could no longer ignore the inner callings of my heart, and that this trip would allow me to step out of the existence I was living in for the better. This ended up being true. Never did I work in a corporate environment again, where I was overworked and not revered for my unique gifts and talents. This trip was vital to me learning how to honor and love myself.

My decision to take this trip and follow my heart's desire didn't stop with merely deciding to embark on the adventure. I also chose to follow my inner guidance on *how* to go about this trip. This was also a bit unorthodox for me. This included the following:

- Not setting a time limit on how long I'd be gone or if I'd return
- Not bringing a phone or communication device with me
- Having a geographic starting point, but no plans thereafter
- Finding one or two communities to live in during my adventure
- Allowing myself not to worry about the future while away

I felt called to start in Southeast Asia, Vietnam specifically. I had been to Thailand the year prior for vacation and fell completely in love with that part of the world. While many friends, colleagues, and family thought I'd lost my mind, I had never felt clearer. This is what it feels like when you are completely in sync with your heart. No matter what the world is showing you or people are telling you, you are clear on your truth. This was one of the most empowering moments of my life.

My trip took me through Vietnam, Cambodia, Laos, India, Malaysia, and Indonesia and it was the experience of a lifetime. I was able to live in Cambodia for three months while volunteering in an orphanage. And, I also lived in Bali, where I had a number of profound spiritual experiences. Despite how atypical it was for me to leave the corporate world at 35 years old—when I was close to the top of the ladder—this trip was the best thing I did for myself. Without it, I wouldn't be doing the work I'm doing today. But more than that, it taught me to trust my heart. It taught me that belief via extraordinary action is what it means to be truly alive.

Herein lies our lesson. Choose to believe in what you want with conviction. Your heart will never lead you down the wrong path. It is there to serve as your guide to true happiness by showing you the path.

Believe in What You Want With Conviction

Why?

Believing in your dreams with conviction is essential to making them a reality. Believing with conviction is devoid of any wishful thinking, which only blocks your desires. Truly believing that what you want is not only possible, but is actually happening, is how strong your conviction needs to be. You want to feel the truth—see it, touch it, feel it and smell it. It's as if it's a reality that's currently happening in another dimension that you're now grabbing onto.

The Practice: Daring to Believe

When you *dare to believe* with conviction, you don't hold anything back. You allow yourself to believe that your deepest desires and dreams are not only possible, but are happening. For this practice, you can use writing, visualization, or both. While you can utilize this practice for any desire, we'll be focusing on your specific soul purpose dream. Once you create the initial visualization in this practice, you'll want to call it forth daily.

What You'll Need

- A journal (optional)
- A pen or pencil (optional)
- A quiet place that enables you to be fully present

How to Do It

Sitting in a quiet place, without distraction, follow these simple steps:

Step 1: Take some deep breaths to center and ground yourself in the moment.

Step 2: Ask your divine guidance of the light and your higher self to help you with opening your heart and mind's eye. Feel free to imagine beautiful white light surrounding you as you say this:

I ask for the highest divine guidance and my higher self to be fully present with me at this time. I ask for your assistance in helping me to open my heart as wide as possible and in allowing my third eye and inner sense of knowing to be completely open and aware in this practice. I ask for your help in allowing me to believe more deeply and fully than I ever have before. According to divine will and for the highest light. And so it is!

Step 3: Next, visualize or write a story that describes, in perfect detail, what your life is like when you're fully living your soul purpose. Whether creating a scene in your mind or writing in your journal, be sure you include the following:

- *What you are specifically doing each day (e.g. if your soul purpose is to be a yoga teacher, then you'd be teaching yoga)*
- *Where you are and who's around you*
- *The things that you're doing with respect to your soul purpose that give you the most joy*
- *How you feel each day*
- *What your life is like—where you live, your environment*
- *What your soul purpose enables you to have (e.g. material, spiritual, emotional)*
- *What it looks like at the apex of your soul purpose (e.g. in love, rich, etc.)*

Step 4: Once you've created the visual in your mind or written the details about your soul purpose, sit with them. Either hold the images in your mind's eye or read aloud what you've written. Feel the bliss as if this has already happened and is true. It may take a while, but try to get yourself to a state of ecstatic bliss. It's helpful at first to sit with the images or keep reading the words until you can generate a level of excitement and joy. From then on, it's easier to recall it.

Step 5: Release the visualization or written copy and ground yourself in the deepest possible level of trust, knowing and belief by saying the following aloud:

I affirm this or better. I ask that the universe now realign circumstances and opportunities according to the highest divine blueprint and timeline for my life, according to divine will. One that allows me to live in unimaginable joy, happiness, and love, as I step fully and completely into my soul purpose. For the highest light and good of all. And so it is!

Choose to believe your dream in your core. It is real and it is happening. It will take some practice. But your belief muscle will strengthen over time. Each day, repeat these steps. Spending about five to ten minutes calling forth this image or reading aloud your description of your soul purpose. Practice believing as if it's already happening, and then releasing it with the prayer.

CHAPTER 7

Living Your Dream

"When you do things from your soul,
you feel a river moving in you, a joy."
- Rumi

After you strengthen your belief muscle in your specific dream, it's time to start living it. This will require that you step into the positive flow of the universe. You will learn how to send a flow of positive energy to your soul purpose and stop the flow of negative energy out of it.

What do I mean by this? First, it's important you understand that we are all co-creators of our realities. Every thought, emotion, and action creates your reality. As the *Law of Attraction*[7] states, it's universal law that like attracts like; you attract into your life what you think about, and more importantly, what you *feel*. But it starts with thought. This is why we have spent so much time discussing the power of fear-based thoughts and beliefs. Every thought you have carries with it a vibrational frequency that's tied to an emotion, which in turn shapes your reality. In other words, living your dreams requires your *conscious participation*.

While a single thought can help to shape an outcome to a momentary experience, collections of thoughts or thought patterns, shape our entire reality. For example, a reactive thought to being stuck in traffic such as, "I'm never going to arrive at my

---

[7] https://en.wikipedia.org/wiki/Law_of_attraction_(New_Thought)

appointment on time," will likely cause stress—a negative vibration—increasing the likelihood that you will be late to your appointment.

Building on that, a collection of negative thoughts in your conscious or subconscious mind such as "Nothing ever works out for me" or "I am just unlucky" will lead to a continual experience of things consistently not going your way, such as being late to appointments. Rather than this being a one-time occurrence, things never working out will become your reality.

Our work in previous chapters on limiting beliefs is foundational to moving into the flow that we are now seeking; until you address the beliefs that correspond to the negative energy that's blocking you, it's nearly impossible to step into positive flow. So, how do you start practicing living in the positive flow of the universe?

1. Accept that you are a powerful co-creator.
2. Direct positive thoughts and emotions toward your dream every day.
3. Notice, pause, and redirect negative thoughts and emotions.

You Are a Co-Creator

Let's take the first one—accepting that you are a powerful co-creator. We spoke about victim consciousness earlier, which is the antitheses of co-creation. When you live in victim consciousness, you view the world as something that is happening to you. That you are subject to the whim of some force that's dictating the reality of your life. You might understand that your actions matter, but the idea that your thoughts and feelings *create* your reality goes right over your head. If any of this sounds familiar to you, even a little bit, it can disrupt being in the flow of your purpose.

For a long time, I didn't realize I had the ability to write the story of my life. I believed there was a predestined version of it that was going to happen regardless of what I did. This is why I did little, for so long, to change the reality of my corporate life. I didn't think there was much I could do. I believed that this was what was destined for me and, as a result, it's what the world presented to me.

But therein lies the truth. The world presented this to me because it was all I had imagined for myself. It was reflective of the low vibrational frequency that I was living in.

Consciously Directing Positive Energy

Sending positive energy to your dream each day is critical to living your soul purpose. This goes beyond intention setting. It's about directing positive thoughts and emotions to your dream. At first, it will be a conscious effort, but as you start to see positive results over time, it will become more innate. For example, when you picture your dream, the goal is to think, "I am so excited…I can't wait!" Feel the excitement and joy because you know it is happening. There should be no question in your mind.

When I first started my purpose work, I wrote a set of positive affirmations about my purpose that I would read aloud every single day. When I recited them, I not only said them with authority, but I also allowed myself to feel the excitement of the dream. My feelings were from a place of deep belief that this was reality, and that it was already happening.

The more we consciously direct positive energy, the more we step into the *universal flow of our purpose* and expand our ability to carry positive energy to all aspects of our life. When we are trapped in negative thinking or feeling, we can thwart our progress or even derail it completely. When you are vibrating in a high frequency, you attract higher vibrational experiences and opportunities. The easiest way to do this is to start before you even get out of bed. Every morning, as soon as I open my eyes, I begin repeating positive thoughts in my mind until I'm so excited I can't wait to start the day. Here are some of my favorites:

I'm going to receive amazing news today.
An unexpected opportunity is flowing my way today.
Everything is working in my favor right now…Everything!
I am a magnet for blessings, miracles and love today.

Redirecting Negative Thinking

We step out of the positive universal flow of co-creation—where everything goes our way and synchronicities are abound—when we have negative thoughts and emotions. To redirect your thinking, you have to be aware of your thoughts. Observing your thoughts and feelings and choosing not to identify with them, *as your truth*, is your first goal. Then, redirect them. This is where meditation can be incredibly helpful. If you don't have a meditation practice, I highly recommend you pick one up. It will help you with all of the lessons in this book, and this one in particular. Being able to observe your thoughts and emotions is key to being able to consciously choose different ones.

Don't put pressure on yourself by expecting this one to be easy off the bat. I still struggle with this lesson to this day. In fact, when I first starting stepping into my purpose, my negative thinking seemed to heighten. I had constant feelings of doubt, jealously, and guilt. At times, I would go from feeling incredibly positive to being overwhelmed with worry. My emotions were a constant seesaw. In particular, when something didn't work out the way I wanted it to, I would look to that as *evidence* that my dream was actually never going to happen. When this happened, I'd fall back into fear and have to revisit some of the lessons in the earlier chapters.

The goal in these moments is to redirect your fearful thinking. An essential part of this is pausing your negative thoughts or emotions as soon as you become aware of them. Take a breath and then direct positive flow energy toward them. Toward your dream. Even if it takes ten minutes or more. Think about having your dream as something that's already happened and let the good feelings flow.

Negative Thinking vs. Healing

The negative thinking I'm referring to above is common, fear-based ego programming. Things we all experience, on some level, as part of the human condition. A self-doubt, worry, or glass half-empty mentality. Whereby, you see yourself and the world, from a limited, small perspective. While you want to work on shifting your "negative beliefs" as they pertain to your soul purpose, also be open to deeper healing that arises.

Redirecting negative thinking doesn't mean ignoring or repressing what needs to be healed within you. We are here to heal. And you definitely have wounds from past experiences that need to be felt, transmuted, and integrated, as part of your healing process. What you repress will only grow, so be sure that by redirecting negative thought patterns, you aren't evading deep wounds or emotions that need to be released as part of your own awakening process.

For example, there is no heavier sensation of pain than when you lose someone close to you. To heal, you must feel the pain of the loss, as unpleasant as it might be. This includes experiencing all of the emotions tied to it, from sadness to anger, which is essential to the process of release. Additionally, if you're having a bad week or month, where you feel depressed and sad and you just can't shake it, this might signify that there is something deeper that needs to be healed. Both of these scenarios represent more than shifting negative thoughts.

How can you tell the difference between negative thinking versus something deeper that needs to be healed? By the *density* of it, both in the *feeling* itself and in its *duration*. When this happens, it's not about redirecting, it's about healing.

Therefore, take notice of any reoccurring patterns of negative thinking, or the duration of a particular feeling, as indicators of deeper wounds that require healing. Notice what your inner guidance is telling you. Where healing is needed, be open to receiving it. Give yourself permission to let it go; don't repress the pain. In fact, the more open you become to healing, transmuting and integrating all aspects of you, the more light you allow in. This is how you step into greater alignment with the divine. More on this in the lesson below as well as in Lesson 10.

Flow Positive Energy Toward Your Purpose

Why?

The universe contains a current of loving, positive energy flow. Living in this energy is essential to manifesting your soul purpose. The universal flow is easy to recognize—it's the frequency of love. Your soul purpose is synonymous with this flow. When you're sending out negative energy, you hinder yourself from being in your soul purpose. That's why learning how to be in the flow is essential. As part of this, recognizing, releasing, and transmuting past pain will be critical.

The Practice: Living in the Flow

When you *live in the flow*, you maintain a high vibrational frequency. At first, this is conscious. Over time, it will become innate. Each day, you will consciously direct positive flow energy to your purpose and redirect negative thinking. For some, this will come quickly, while for others, it will take practice. Either way, it's the conscious intention in this exercise that matters most.

What You'll Need

- A journal
- A pen or pencil
- A quiet place that enables you to be fully present

How to Do It

This exercise has several steps. First, we need to tackle any remaining doubts you have about your ability to co-create. From there, we can get into the practice. As with the other lessons, make sure you are in a quiet place, where you can be fully present.

Step 1: As always, take some deep grounding breaths and invite in divine guidance and your higher self to guide you in this practice.

Step 2: Address the limiting beliefs you have around co-creation. If you have any doubts about your ability to co-create your dream, use the format from our earlier lesson on limiting beliefs to tackle them head-on. List them first, then identify the root cause and explore what would happen if it weren't true. Finally, write a new belief.

Feel free to also apply the subconscious mind release from Lesson 5. Here are some common limiting beliefs around co-creation to help guide you.

Limiting Beliefs	Root Cause	What If This Wasn't True	New Belief
I am not a co-creator.			
Co-creation isn't real.			
Co-creation isn't possible.			
It's hard work to co-create.			
I can't co-create everything.			
God is in charge not me.			

Step 3: Once you've addressed the core beliefs and blocks you have around your ability to co-create, it's time to get into the practice of flowing positive energy. I recommend when you are first getting started with this practice to leverage positive affirmations, three to five at a time. Describe the details of how each makes you feel. A good affirmation is about already having the thing you want. Here are some examples:

- *I am an inspirational speaker and spiritual teacher who is creating a world of abundance via soul purpose for every human being.*

- *I'm a best-selling author and wellness expert who is awakening the world to better health and holistic options.*
- *As a full-time yoga teacher, I'm paid more money than I ever imagined and I feel empowered, happy, and healthy.*

Step 4: Once you have your affirmations written, practice saying them out loud each day and feeling the exuberance, joy, and excitement as if these things have already happened. Repeat, shout, affirm them and feel the pure joy and happiness that fills your soul.

Step 5: Throughout the day, consciously send positive energy to your dream. Bring up the image of the dream in your mind, see it clearly and feel the immense happiness you feel when you have what you want.

Step 6: Intend each day to observe when you're having negative thoughts and emotions about your purpose. When you are, just pause. Then, consciously redirect positive energy toward your dream following the step above.

If the negative thought or emotion is tied to something deeper within you that requires healing, please move onto the step below. If not, you can stop here. Trust your inner guidance to advise you in this process. If you're feeling a gentle nudge that this is about a deeper wound, trust that voice.

Step 7: There is no simple answer to healing your inner wounds. What I've found is that a willingness to feel your pain, as well as a willingness to let go of it, is what it takes to initiate the healing process. Here's an overview of how I approach my own wounds:

- **Feel Them:** Allow yourself to sit with the pain, wound or whatever is coming up for you and *feel* deeply into it; all the injury and trauma that has caused your pain. Cry, scream, do whatever you need to do—let it out.

- **Be Willing:** Ask yourself if you're *really* willing to release this pain. You might need to first acknowledge the ways in which it currently serves you if you aren't 100% willing. Affirm your willingness to heal.

- **Ask for Help:** Once you're willing, ask the divine/God/Source/energy to help you release it. State that you are willing to release it and ask for direct assistance to do so, according to divine will. Ask to be shown the way and affirm you are willing to be guided step-by-step.

- **Release It:** Give yourself permission to release your pain in this moment. Feel free to do the prayer and visualization in the next step to aid in the release, transmutation, and integration of your wounds. Also, be open to any gentle nudges or guidance you are receiving about what you need to do to release this pain wholly and completely. Trust, and take the action you are being guided to take.

Step 8: Prayer and visualization is a powerful form of release. You may use the prayer and healing technique below, which is based in part, on energetic principles of self-healing. As such, use your imagination when you do this prayer, as an active participant in the process. Suggested ideas of what you can visualize while doing this prayer are in *parentheses*. However, please allow your own imagination to facilitate this process, as best you can.

I call on divine source and my higher self to be with me now as I ask for your help in releasing (state wound). I affirm that I am completely ready to heal this part of myself (visualize a white light all around you). I now ask for this wound to be completely released from my mental, emotional, physical, and spiritual bodies (imagine a dark smoke or grey cloud leaving you and choose to consciously feel it leaving you). Please take all of this pain and inner turmoil and transmute it wholly and completely into light and love (imagine a beautiful violet light transmuting this dark smoke into radiant white light). And I ask that my higher self, please return this soul energy to me, once it's completely healed, at the right time, and according to divine will. And so it is!

This exercise is just one way that you can work towards healing your deeper wounding. There are many practices and modalities in which to explore healing yourself. Entire books are dedicated to just this topic. If this is an area you feel called to do more work in, I recommend exploring any one of the many books on *shadow work*[8].

In summary, this lesson is about the practice of maintaining a consistent high vibrational frequency. To do this, become a conscious observer of your frequency level throughout the day. Do you feel light or do you feel weighed down by heaviness and density? An easy way to notice this is to schedule three to five *self-checks* throughout the day, where you take a moment to pause and assess how you're feeling. Send yourself re-occurring calendar invites to make it easy.

The more you can consciously choose positive thoughts and emotions, the quicker you'll manifest your dreams. Over time, living in a higher vibration will become normal for you. But at first, you must make this a conscious practice. Choose positive thoughts and feelings over negative ones. And, be willing to release what needs to go.

---

[8] Robert A. Johnson, Owning Your Own Shadow: Understanding the Dark Side of the Psyche, 2009; Debbie Ford, The Secret of the Shadow, 2009.

CHAPTER 8

Take Inspired Action

*"Action without vision is only passing time,
vision without action is merely day dreaming, but
vision with action can change with world."*
- Nelson Mandela

Taking daily inspired actions is how you manifest your soul purpose into being. Inspired action isn't linear and it's not a well-thought out action plan. Quite the opposite. Inspired actions come from the universe via messages, signs—a gut feeling. It's the language of universal guidance that only wants to help you manifest your dream into being. Your job is to remain present enough to see, hear, or feel it, then take an inspired action based upon it.

Inspired Actions vs. Action Plan

Inspired actions, which come as messages from the divine, can feel a bit far-fetched, particularly if you are a linear thinker like me. I'm someone who was always accustomed to having a plan. This action plan was process-oriented, with a series of steps, timelines, and goals. There was little flexibility in it. It was always about sticking to the plan! As a matter of fact, having a step-by-step course of action was my guarantee. I hadn't realized at the time that needing a guarantee was just another way of holding onto the underlying belief that my dreams weren't possible. My lack of faith manifested as the need for a plan.

What I came to learn, through much difficulty, is that this type of approach isn't how the universe works when it comes to manifesting soul purpose. As much as your purpose is a heart-centered endeavor, so are the actions you need to take to manifest it into being. This means you have to let go of *how* your purpose will manifest into being as well as any expectation of timing. You don't sacrifice the clarity of your vision, just the *how*. Trusting and collaborating with the universe is how you make your dream a reality. It can also be one of the hardest things to do.

Trusting in the Universe

Learning to trust in the universe comes back to belief. Belief is something that at first, you simply choose. For many, strong, unwavering beliefs come after years of having direct experience with seeing your beliefs rewarded. This is part of the human thought process—we need evidence first.

I, myself had a powerful experience when I first started stepping into the manifestation of my soul purpose. In 2016, I started a company that was the symbolic representation of my soul purpose. The company name were my initials, JLJ.

In the first year of running the company, I was plagued by constant fear and doubt. I was trying to manage everything myself and hadn't yet put my trust into the universe. After enough disappointment and as part of my own spiritual awakening, I started to practice co-creating with the universe by trusting I was being guided and taking inspired action.

In the summer of 2016, I was having a particularly tough time. I felt lost and uncertain about my future. So, I asked the universe to guide me via a direct sign about whether or not I should continue trying to build JLJ or whether I should give up and find a job that offered security. During a very distraught week, I continually asked the universe for this guidance, not really believing the universe was listening.

One night while I was walking home from work, I received my

answer. I was about a block from my apartment in the West Village. Sad and distraught, I was weeping hopelessly. As I was crossing the street, I looked down by chance and saw the letters JLJ on a metal plate that was covering some construction work on the street. I was so shocked that I paused to be sure if I was seeing what I thought I was seeing. Was this really a message from the universe or was I losing my mind?

The next morning, I walked back and the plate was still there with the letters JLJ clearly engraved on it. I then looked around and saw that the name of the construction company doing the work was also JLJ. In fact, there was other construction equipment on the street that also had the letters JLJ on it. That explained it! This wasn't a message from the universe; it was just a coincidence. Phew, I wasn't going crazy!

But it was then that a small voice inside reminded me that there are no coincidences. This voice gently suggested to me to not mistake this for a coincidence but instead to see it as the divine guidance I'd been seeking. And the message was clear: Have faith in my business, in my dream.

It was in this moment that I knew I had a choice. I could experience life believing everything is just chance and random occurrence, that there is no divine guidance at play...Or I could choose to believe in the magic of the universe—a loving guidance that's always at play, where miracles aren't only possible, but real. This was my opportunity to decide which world I wanted to live in. Knowing that my decision, either way, would impact the reality I would experience moving forward. The answer was clear. I chose to live in a world where miracles are real and where the universe is helping and guiding me every step of the way.

What world do you choose to live in? If, like me, you want to live in a world where you are surrounded by love and guidance, try repeating these affirmations aloud now and seeing how it feels.

I choose to believe the universe is guiding me.

I choose to believe the universe has my back.

I choose to believe the universe exudes a loving, helpful energy.

I chose this to be the world I wanted to live in because I believe it's the world I *do* live in. And I believe that message delivered was to me from the divine.

How Inspired Action Works

Once you have asked the universe for what you want, the universe will send you help via hunches, gentle nudges and signs. Think of this guidance like breadcrumbs. In other words, you aren't going to receive a letter in the mail from God with your action plan and timing spelled out perfectly. Instead, you are going to receive hunches that you might typically ignore or fail to notice. Your job is to notice them and take action based on them. No matter how insignificant, irrelevant, or strange they seem, your job is to pay attention and act on the bits of guidance you're given.

What does guidance look like? This is a question I'm often asked. Sometimes, it comes in the form that I described earlier with the message about JLJ. But more typically, it comes in the form of hunches. Someone might pop into your mind whom you haven't thought of in a while, and that person may somehow be related to the dream you're trying to manifest. Perhaps they know someone who can help you. Or, you might be inspired or feel compelled to go to a particular gathering or networking event. At this meeting, you receive an important lead for your business.

In short, positive ideas, inspiration and even urges about your life purpose are going to pop into your mind. They feel exciting, positive and good. They do not feel like "chores." Don't judge these ideas or moments of inspiration. Simply take action using your hunches as a leader and see where you end up. After that action, yet another hunch will appear and you'll then take action based on that one.

Once you have manifested your purpose, you'll be able to look backwards and see a perfectly aligned step-by-step plan that was always underway. The challenge is that you won't see this plan while it's ahead of you. This is part of the process and also part of learning to be in the flow of the divine, as inspired action is about deepening your experience of living in the universal flow of co-creation.

Taking inspired action also requires us to stay positive while pausing and redirecting negative thinking when needed. Central to most of our ability to do this is *learning to trust* as well as *making the choice to trust* when it doesn't come naturally. With that, you must release the need to know *how* your dream is going to come into being. Instead, just trust that it will.

Inspired Action vs. Ego Action

The way to think about taking inspired action versus ego-based action is to visualize the energy behind each move you make. Are you taking an action based in a nudge that comes from the energy of love or fear? Here are some examples of the difference:

- Inspired action makes you **feel good**, whereas ego action makes you **feel fearful**.
- Inspired action is usually **spontaneous**, whereas ego action is a **result of thinking how to make things happen**.
- Inspired action comes when you are **simply allowing**, while ego action comes from a **need to control**.
- Inspired action can feel **exciting and motivating**, while ego action feels **stressful or burdensome**.

The most important thing is to try and have fun with this and release all ties to outcome. When you feel yourself in the energy of fear or control, you're not taking inspired action. You're out of the positive universal flow of co-creation. But know it takes practice. Do not be hard on yourself with this part of your journey. Take comfort in knowing that even my own practice of this continues to be a work in progress.

I remember when someone once said something similar to me, I thought, "Well, if I mess this part up, I'm not going to manifest my purpose, right?" The answer is no. This is not an obstacle course or test you have to master to get what you want. Remember our earlier work on limiting beliefs? The universe isn't cruel. It didn't give you a desire and the courage to ask for what you want without being committed to helping you realize it. That's not how this works.

Every time you feel in doubt, frustrated, or scared about manifesting your purpose, re-center on the knowledge that the universe is here to help. Any time you feel you've gotten out of positive flow, that's okay. Pause and jump right back in with excitement and joy, knowing you have the best possible teammate helping you to make your dreams come true. The universe wants to see you succeed and is pulling out all the stops for you.

Inspired Action is the Key to Manifesting Your Soul Purpose

Why?

Inspired action comes from your higher self. The part of the universe that's connected to your soul. Therefore, when it comes to soul purpose, there is no better guidance than your own gut feeling for manifesting your dream into being. When we get into the mindset of trying to figure things out and make them happen, we are acting from our ego. Our ego isn't interested in us living our soul purpose. So, naturally, relying on our ego self to help bring our dream to fruition can delay or block our manifestation results.

The Practice: Taking Inspired Action

When you *take inspired action* you pay attention to the gentle nudges, hunches, and even signs that the universe is sending you. You can then take an inspired action based on these nudges. Inspired action is about staying in the moment and having trust. It is not about having a plan as to exactly *how* your dream is going to become real. Can you have a plan around inspired actions that arise? Of course. But you have to be willing to toss it out as soon as you feel you're out of flow with the universe. The idea is to stay trusting in the flow of the universe and to release the idea that *you* are responsible for making your dream happen or that *you* need to will it into being, which is the mentality of ego-based action, not inspired action.

What You'll Need

- A conscious decision to trust the universe

- To start, a quiet place where you can be fully present

How to Do It

This exercise is all about being in the moment and getting to a place where you can feel comfortable in the flow of taking inspired action toward your vision on a daily basis. In this practice, your vision is clear; you surrender the how. To start, set some time aside each morning to sit with yourself in quiet resonance, to hear your inner guidance and set an intention of inspired action with regard to your vision for that day. Then, with practice, you can simply live this exercise moment-to-moment as part of living your purpose.

Step 1: In the morning, sit quietly and take several deep, centering breaths. Really focus on grounding and dropping into your heart center. You can visualize your heart opening and your higher self dropping from above and entering the sacred space of your heart. Set your intention with the universe. Here's an example:

> *I ask the universe to help guide and assist me in manifesting my purpose today. Please show me exactly what actions to take today via hunches, gentle nudges, and clear signs. Please assist me in noticing your divine guidance and taking inspired action based on it. According to divine will. And so it is!*

Step 2: While you're in this quiet space, ask, "What is my next step toward manifesting my purpose?" Sit quietly and listen for the answer. Whatever thought, idea, nudge, or hunch comes to you is your answer. Don't judge it or censor it. Simply observe it.

Step 3: Take the action that you feel most inspired to take based on the nudge you have received. Be sure to take the action that day; don't postpone.

Step 4: Repeat this process each morning. However, be open to receiving guidance all day long. As you receive guidance throughout the day, take the action within 24 hours.

Step 5: Be sure, especially at first, that you're not taking ego action. If you're not sure whether a nudge is coming from your higher self or the universe, as opposed to your ego, here's a quick checklist you can use to evaluate:

- Does the guidance feel loving or fearful?
- Does it feel exciting or stressful?
- Is it unexpected or something you've figured out?

As you get into the flow of living in inspired action, you may want to skip the formality of the morning intention ritual. That's fine. Just be sure to stay in conscious awareness of the energy of your guidance and actions. If you feel yourself slipping back into the energy of fear and negativity, incorporate the morning ritual back into your routine and repeat as much as needed.

CHAPTER 9

Be Courageous with Your Actions

"Courage isn't something to muster;
it's something to allow."
- Yours truly

When you decide to live your soul purpose, expect courageous action to be a part of what you're guided to do. In reality, the actions you take aren't courageous per se, in that you're not facing any real risk, but they will seem courageous because they are likely to be *different* than what you're used to doing.

Most of us live in the safe haven of the ego, where we make safe choices based on perceived fears. In the beginning, courage will be required to take a different course. In time and with continuous dedication, like with many of the other lessons, this way of being will become a part of who you are.

What is the Ego?

I've mentioned the ego or ego self throughout our lessons. Let's discuss the ego more now. Many spiritual teachings and religions cast the ego as the enemy—something to be feared and conquered. I've found from personal experience that this type of thinking is not helpful. It can even make the problem, which you perceive as ego, stronger.

When I first started digging deep into my own soul purpose manifestation work, I thought my objective was to quiet the ego, by whatever means necessary, and hear my true self. This is in part true. As I practiced this, however, my ego voice started becoming louder. As a result, I started viewing my ego as the enemy, something to be conquered. This only exacerbated things and made my recovery process all the more strenuous.

That's because there's nothing more ego-driven than the idea of battling or conquering, which is typical terminology used in popular culture when people are confronted with a challenge. What happened as a result of trying to suppress my ego is that my ego voice became louder and more challenging. I was feeding it exactly what it wanted. I entered a state of anger and negativity. What I've come to learn since then is that you actually have to *love the ego* if you really want to quiet it.

The ego is a like a small, scared child. A self-made construct we create to help us survive in a world that we perceive as scary. It's not some evil force we have no control over. We created it, therefore, with work, we can control the importance it plays in our lives. In fact, we can choose to make decisions or take actions based on what our ego is telling us.

I've often been advised to think of the ego like a collection of computer programs that we have developed to make sense of a scary world.[9] We create these programs to protect ourselves based on a false interpretation of the word. We each have created our own unique programs based on our individual life experiences. We also have programs based on the larger collective consciousness. Notions like "Death is scary" or "There are not enough natural resources" are programs to which the vast majority of people subscribe. No matter what the program, the goal is the same: *Reinforce fears based on illusion.*

One of the best ways to practice quieting the ego is through

---

[9] Steve Nobel, The Soul Matrix, www.thesoulmatrix.com

meditation, which I've suggested several times in this book. My favorite type of mediation is *mantra meditation*. If you are new to this type of meditation, please check out Deepak Chopra's Ananda meditation app[10] for an introduction. Regardless which practice you use, in meditation, one of the key benefits is learning to observe your thoughts without attachment. Without one, it's likely that the majority of the thoughts you are conscious of throughout the day come from your ego self vs. higher self.

Higher Self vs. Ego

To understand your ego voice on an even deeper level, compare it to pure consciousness. The higher self is pure conscious awareness, whereas the ego is all about illusion—primarily, the illusion of separation. The ego voice will tell you that you're separate from other living beings, divine love, and the universe. But your higher self knows that this isn't true. It communicates the truth to you, that the only real truth is the universal consciousness of love. We are all, in fact, one.

Here's an example of how this illusion can play out in everyday life. When the ego self walks on a busy sidewalk, it sees everyone as separate, perhaps even as a threat. It applies an us-versus-them mode of thinking. When the higher self takes the same walk, it sees itself in everyone it meets. It sees the love that is in everyone and understands that we are all connected.

When you get into manifesting your soul purpose, your higher self and ego self will weigh in on every action and decision you make—especially the big decisions that come up. The ego will show you everything that can go wrong, while your higher self will be a voice of encouragement and support. Your job will be to decipher the action that's aligned to the higher self and follow its lead.

------

[10] Chopra Center, Ananda App Download: https://chopraananda.com/

Take my decision to spend a year traveling instead of working. My heart was telling me this was the right thing to do for myself at the time. My head (AKA ego) was telling me that this was a crazy idea and presenting a long list of reasons about how this could backfire and ruin my life. Or, take when I surrendered to my addiction and got help. In that moment, my head was telling me that my life would be completely over if I got sober, while my heart told me it would be a beautiful new beginning.

In both these moments, I had a choice to make: listen to my heart or listen to my head.

Because I wasn't versed in following my heart, that approach felt scary and risky. In both these moments, I simply had to allow myself to be courageous. To not think twice about it. Was it courageous to follow my heart? On the surface, yes. It is courageous to face your fears and not to be ruled by them. But in actuality, taking any action based on what your heart is telling you to do is the safest path. But because we are so used to living in illusion and doing what our ego tells us to do, when you first start following your heart via taking extraordinary action, it will require courage. In time, however, it will become more comfortable.

LESSON 9:

———————————————

Let Courage Define You...
Until it Becomes You

Why?

The universe is going to guide you to take action and make big decisions that the ego perceives as frightening. While there is nothing safer you can do than follow the guidance of your heart, courage will be required. With practice, making decisions and taking action based on the guidance of the heart will become more normal and less intimidating. The courage first required to follow this path will simply become a part of who you are.

The Practice: Allowing Courage

When you *allow courage* to inform critical actions on your purpose journey, you are choosing to ignore the fear and listen to the higher self, which speaks to you through love. This is similar to our last lesson in terms of identifying and following inspired, universal action, instead of ego-derived action. However, this practice can be applied when you're feeling stuck because the fear is so great.

What You'll Need

- Your journal
- A pen or pencil
- To start, a quiet place where you can be fully present

How to Do It

Use this exercise when you are feeling stuck over a decision or choice you need to make with regard to manifesting your soul purpose. No matter how big or small, if you're at a fork in the road and unable to stay in the flow of where the universe is guiding you, use this practice to overcome your fear and get back into flow.

Step 1: As always, center yourself and ask for help by closing your eyes and taking a few deep grounding breaths. Call in for help and guidance from the universe and your higher self by reciting this to yourself:

I now ask for divine guidance from the highest light to help me make a decision that is for my greatest good and helps me to continue on the highest path to manifesting my divine soul purpose.

Step 2: Make a table with three columns. In the left, write what the decision or choice is that you have been inspired to take by the universe. A few examples are listed below.

Potential Decision		
To travel for a year and not work		
To start my own business		
To write a book		

Step 3: List the biggest fears you have about taking this action. This is your ego guidance. Take note of any that are tied to your core limiting beliefs and be sure to incorporate into the work you have done from Lesson 5.

Potential Decision	Ego Based Guidance	
To travel for a year and not work	I'll lose all my money I'll lose my place on the corporate ladder Everyone will think I'm crazy	
To start my own business	I don't have enough support I'm not resourceful enough I have a family to support	
To write a book	I don't have the time I'm not a good enough writer Nobody makes money off of books Getting published is hard	

Step 4: Next, list the guidance from your higher self about this decision. If you're having trouble distinguishing or hearing your higher self, close your eyes and put your hand over your heart. Then, ask for clear guidance. Remember, your higher self speaks to you through love. Anything that is fear-based is your ego.

Potential Decision	Ego Based Guidance	Higher Self Guidance
Whether to travel for a year and not work	I'll lose all my money I'll lose my place on the corporate ladder I'll miss out on beneficial opportunities Everyone will think I'm crazy	This will be good for my soul There will always be a job waiting for me This is what is needed for my health This will be the best thing I ever do I deserve this
Whether to start a business	I don't have enough support I'm not resourceful enough I have a family to support	My business will be successful This will make me truly happy I will have many clients
Whether to write a book	I don't have the time I'm not a good enough writer Nobody makes money off of books Getting published is hard	The world is waiting to hear my words People will be helped by my book My book will be a best seller My book will get published

Step 5: Here's where allowing courage in comes into play. In these moments, you have a choice. You can choose to listen to your ego guidance and make a decision based on what it has to say. Or, you can listen to your higher guidance and choose to trust in it. The choice is yours, but know that only one is aligned to your soul purpose path. That's why in this moment, it's about *leaping* when your higher self says to.

Step 6: If you are having a hard time allowing the courage to flow and taking the action that's aligned with your heart, here are a few tactics you can try:

- Ask the universal light and your higher self to help you muster the courage you need to leap forward in line with the heart-centered action
- If you're feeling lost or overwhelmed by the decision, break down the heart-centered action into a series of baby steps
    - Ask for help with allowing courage to take each step
    - Then, take one step at a time with courage until you're onto the next

Always do your best to move forward with your heart-centered action no matter how much fear you feel. Sometimes, you just have to leap.

CHAPTER 10

Confront Resistance Head-on

"Ego trip: a journey to nowhere."
- Robert Half

Resistance on your path stems from the ego. That's why we've spent so much time talking about it. The ego is not to be feared, but actively recognized. We all have an ego. In fact, the human experience is dominated by it. Allowing your higher self to lead is a lifelong skill that you must develop.

The ego actually has your best interest at heart from its limited perspective. The ego believes it's protecting you. Through deeply loving the ego, you diminish the power you've anointed it. The more you're able to do this, the more easily you can submit to your highest life purpose.

Below are a few ways in which your ego self will try to protect you as you walk along your soul purpose path. There is nothing to be alarmed about when these emotions and constructs arise. It's a normal part of the process. The goal is to be aware of them when they do arise. This will serve to reduce your self-created resistance to achieving your soul purpose. It will also help to illuminate parts of you that require healing.

Guilt

This is an emotion that can be intense, especially when you have a lot of people who are dependent on you or if you've suffered any kind of abuse in your lifetime (physical, verbal, financial, or otherwise). The ego likes to tell us that doing something that fulfills our soul is actually harming those around us. There couldn't be anything further from the truth. However, when you're used to allowing guilt to influence your actions and decisions, it can be quite uncomfortable at first to step out of it.

I experienced guilt in 2011 when I traveled to Asia. I felt bad that I was away from my family for so long. But I also felt guilty that I was taking time off from work to enjoy myself. Guilty to whom in particular? I didn't even know. Something just felt inherently wrong and selfish in doing it, particularly at that age.

I've also felt immense guilt over those I hurt when I was in active addiction. It took me a long time to have compassion for the disease and to not continue to carry that guilt into my relationships during sobriety. This included feeling proud to put my sobriety above all else and learning to include my loved ones in my sobriety process after neglecting some of them for so long. When in reality, there is nothing better I could do for myself or those around me.

The truth about guilt is that it keeps us imprisoned in a cycle. This can be a cycle of addiction, abuse, of poverty, or even of poor health. In this case, guilt is serving to keep you from living what your heart really wants. The only way to overcome this is to acknowledge the guilt and take action *in spite of the guilt*. Like our prior lessons, at first it will feel uncomfortable, but it will get easier with time.

Is this to say we should quit our jobs with no immediate tangible possibility of income when we have a family to support? Certainly not. And our higher self won't guide us to do this. The point is to be aware of the ways in which guilt is keeping you in a cycle of resistance from realizing your soul purpose dreams. Because these patterns of resistance are most likely stemming from your ego.

Self-doubt

This is the number one area of resistance for me. Self-doubt is tied to an *expectation of perfectionism*. When this shows up, it's really about an incorrect definition the ego has about the world. In the ego's eyes, we need to be perfect because we need to be in control at all times in order to compensate for a universe (and us, by association) that is flawed.

We must reverse this flaw of the ego! The universe is always in divine working order, but because the ego doesn't understand how this divine order works, it interprets what it doesn't understand as imperfection. It sees chaos where there is actually divine synchronicity. This is because the ego isn't designed to see the bigger picture.

The best way to alleviate self-doubt is to remind yourself that you are a powerful spiritual being with immense capabilities. As you remind yourself of this, do so with compassion for the ego, who isn't able to see you for who you really are. Another way to diminish feelings of self-doubt is to embrace vulnerability. Practice admitting when you feel scared, don't know the answer, or just feel perplexed or lost. It's okay. In fact, there is no better way to quiet the resistance of self-doubt than to take pride in your outspoken, at times clumsy or uncomfortable, vulnerability.

Jealousy

I struggle with jealousy quite often, which is tied to my limiting belief around scarcity. When I started JLJ, I experienced a lot of jealousy from others who were seemingly successful. But my jealously was just my ego saying to me:

There's a limit to the number of people who can do what you do.
You can't create what you want.
Competitors are real and they are a threat to your dreams.

When you notice yourself feeling jealous of others, remember that it's a good sign that others have what you want. This means it is indeed possible; it's a profound signal. When you notice yourself being jealous of people who are living your soul purpose dream, simply pause and observe that it must mean the universe needs what you have to offer. In fact, you can thank the universe for reminding you that you are close to attaining what you want.

Disappointment

Disappointment is usually tied to something not working out in the way you thought it would. While we're going to talk more about surrendering to outcomes in the next chapter, it's important to highlight that disappointment is how resistance will likely show up the most. When you feel disappointed it's the same as saying to the universe, "I never get what I want." If this is the energy you put out, you're likely receive it in return.

I struggle with disappointment immensely. Before I had learned how to practice having conviction in my beliefs, I was constantly looking for evidence that my dreams didn't have a chance of becoming real. Everything that didn't work out the way I thought it should—every ostensible disappointment—kept me in a state of avoidance of my purpose. When I didn't get a client I thought I should have gotten or the recognition I thought I deserved, I would let my disappointment get the best of me. This would take me back several steps on progress I'd made toward my purpose.

Disappointment is what happens when we take things too seriously. We view each point on our journeys as fixed rather than always moving and in flux. We forget that co-creation is very much a game—an experience of joyful play with the divine. The more you embrace and incorporate play into your soul purpose journey, loving the tenuous nature of things, will you release the pressure valve that leads to disappointment.

Additionally, letting go of any expectation of outcome is critical to overcoming this form of resistance. When I'm disappointed, I first allow myself to feel it, then I release it, knowing that rejection is also the universe's way of protecting me. Hence the saying: "Rejection is God's protection." Further, perceived disappointment is a gentle reminder that part of the fun is we don't know how our purpose will exactly manifest or evolve, but the universe does. So you can relax and let the universe take its course.

Impatience

Similarly to disappointment, impatience operates as form of resistance that our ego presents to us. Like disappointment, impatience is tied to an *expectation of time*. Remember that manifesting our dreams doesn't happen overnight, but they will come true. As mentioned earlier, the universe doesn't place dreams in our heart to torture us. They are there to be fulfilled. However, having respect for divine timing is paramount to living your soul purpose.

Back to JLJ, in those days, I allowed my ego to convince me that success should have happened much quicker than it did. Similarly to how I used disappointment as evidence to prove to a skeptical ego that my dreams were possible, I used time as an excuse to forfeit. When things weren't going quickly or according to the schedule I had laid out for myself, my ego took it as proof that my dream wouldn't manifest and that I was being silly in thinking that it would. Clearly, I had work to do on strengthening my belief muscle.

When you feel impatient, it's best to remind yourself that you don't actually know how long it will take to manifest your purpose. But know that feeling impatient certainly isn't helping to accelerate it. In this moment, consciously surrender all timelines to the universe while reaffirming your trust.

As with our work in Lesson 7, patterns of resistance that are on repeat may signal deeper healing that needs to happen. Take notice and ask for divine guidance to help you look within and understand any bigger pain patterns that need to be addressed.

Release All Forms of Resistance

Why?

It's rare to go through the process of manifesting your dreams without being confronted by different forms of resistance from the ego. This is simply part of the journey. Being aware of all the ways resistance shows up and quickly releasing them will ensure you stay on your path toward living your dream. It also allows you to notice potential patterns of deeper wounds that need addressing.

The Practice: Resistance Release

Awareness of resistance is the most important step in not letting it control you and disrupt your ability to manifest. Practicing *resistance release* is greatly aided by having a strong meditation practice. Additionally, identifying all the ways in which resistance shows up for you will help you to not be derailed by it. That way, when it shows up, you simply acknowledge what it is *and* what it isn't. Then, you do a simple release exercise. This practice should be leveraged any time resistance is showing up while you manifest your purpose into being.

What You'll Need

- Your journal
- A pen or pencil
- To start, a quiet place where you can be fully present
- Meditation app unless you already have a meditation practice

How to Do It

Meditation is something you should practice every day to help alleviate ego resistance. That's why it's the first step in this practice. The following steps can then be used whenever forms of resistance show up.

Daily practice

Meditation will aid all the lessons in this book, as referenced several times. If you're just starting out, I recommend using one of the many meditation apps that are available. I recommend Deepak Chopra's Ananda meditation app, which you can download here at chopraananda.com. You should meditate every morning for a minimum of 10 minutes.

Resistance Release

Step 1: As always, close your eyes and take some deep grounding breaths to center yourself. Call in your highest guidance to help guide you in this process:

> *The highest divine guidance of light and love…I ask you to be with me now to help me see how resistance is showing up and blocking me from living my soul purpose.*

Step 2: Make a table with three columns. In the left column, identify the areas of resistance that are showing up, using the list below as an example. Add any that you are experiencing, even if not listed in these examples.

Areas of Resistance			
Guilt			
Shame			
Disappointment			
Jealousy			
Impatience			
Judgement			

Self-pity			
Doubt			

Step 3: Identify how each form of resistance serves your ego's mission to protect you from your soul purpose.

Areas of Resistance	How it Serves My Ego	The Truth	
Guilt	It will hurt others if I take action		
Blame	I am not a co-creator		
Disappointment	Confirms I never get what I want		
Jealousy	What I want to do is limited		
Impatience	Confirms it's just too long and hard to do		
Judgement	Others are a threat to my dreams		
Self-Pity	Nothing works out for me		
Doubt	My dreams aren't possible		

Step 4: Now, add in the truth as your higher self knows it. If you need help hearing the guidance of your higher self, close your eyes, place your hand over your heart and ask for help.

Areas of Resistance	How it Serves My Ego	The Truth	
Guilt	It will hurt others if I take action	Keeps me out of positive action	
Blame	I am not a co-creator	I am a powerful co-creator	
Disappointment	Confirms I never get what I want	I know my dreams are possible	
Jealousy	What I want to do is finite	This shows me my dream is possible	
Impatience	Confirms it's just too long and hard to do	I can trust divine timing	
Judgement	Others are a threat to my dreams	Judging others only hurts myself	
Self-Pity	Nothing works out for me	Everything is working in my favor	
Doubt	My dreams aren't possible	All my dreams are possible	

Step 5: Finally, if any of these forms of resistance seems to be repeating itself, explore whether it's a part of deeper wounds you have that require healing.

Areas of Resistance	How it Serves My Ego	The Truth	Tied to Deeper Wounding?
Guilt	It will hurt others if I take action	Keeps me out of positive action	Yes, my guilt around being an addict.
Blame	I am not a co-creator	I am a powerful co-creator	No
Disappointment	Confirms I never get what I want	I know my dreams are possible	No
Jealousy	What I want to do is finite	This shows me my dream is possible	No.
Impatience	Confirms it's just too long and hard to do	I can trust divine timing	No.
Judgement	Others are a threat to my dreams	Judging others only hurts myself	No.
Self-Pity	Nothing works out for me	Everything is working in my favor	Yes, my self-pity from feeling like a victim.
Doubt	My dreams aren't possible	All my dreams are possible	No.

For any wounds you identify, return to Steps 7 and 8 in Lesson 7.

Step 6: When any areas of resistance show up for you, quickly remind yourself of how they are serving your ego and what the *higher truth* actually is.

Step 7: Restate your commitment to your purpose and ask for these areas of resistance to be released as often as they arise. You can also incorporate this release prayer into your morning routine as you start your day.

I now confirm my conviction and belief that my dream of X is happening. I know it with every ounce of my soul. I ask for assistance from the universe to help me release all resistance permanently and completely from my conscious and subconscious minds. I now affirm that they no longer hold any power over me as I align completely with my higher self. And so it is!

Remember that when resistance shows up, it's actually a great sign! It means that you are on your path to living your soul purpose. Otherwise, you would not be confronted with pushback from the ego. In situations that feel particularly debilitating, remind yourself of this important fact. You are actually closer than you think.

CHAPTER 11

Surrender All Outcomes to the Divine

"I do not understand the mystery of grace —
only that it meets us where we are but does
not leave us where it found us."
- Anne Lamott

It might sound strange, after talking about the power of believing in your dreams and co-creating the life that you want, to follow that by saying it's also necessary to *surrender all outcomes to the divine*. When I first came across this idea, I felt utterly and wholly confused.

Here was my logic: I need to have a clear vision for my dreams and focus on becoming a co-creator, but I shouldn't care whether my wishes actually come to fruition? What?! You've got to be kidding me!

Well, not at all actually. In fact, this is exactly how it works.

Here's the thing about human existence: We have an innate need to control outcomes because of the fear-based programming we have created to help us cope. Going back to prior chapters, remember that this need to control is a form of negative energy. When we attach the fear of not getting what we want to our desired outcomes, we likely ensure we won't get what we want. Therefore, doing the work but surrendering to the outcome is key to living your soul purpose.

Again, it took me a long time to wrap my head around this one. Because in reality, these are the steps you must take:

1. Get clear on what you want.
2. Ask the universe for what you want.
3. Believe what you want is possible.
4. Coordinate with the universe to manifest what you want.
5. *Then, surrender to everything you want!*

Makes no sense, right? That's what my highly analytical mind couldn't understand for a long time. But I eventually got it, which is why I know you can, too.

Surrendering attachment to all outcomes is one of the most fulfilling steps to living your soul purpose. When you do it, you'll be at ease and at peace. However, it also tends to be the most challenging step for many.

Who wants to surrender what they want? Let alone to a universe that at times they don't fully understand and know? This can feel like an incredibly intimidating task. But the more you let go, the more love you are actually inviting in. Start with just a little bit of trust and the rest will flourish. And *grace* is the fuel that will guide you there.

State of Grace

Divine grace is always there, whether or not you realize it. The degree to which it encompasses your reality is, in part, up to you. The more you invite grace in, the stronger its presence becomes in your world. When you consciously choose to see grace all around you, your experience and interaction with the world will start to change.

When you first start to notice grace, it might transpire in the form of "miracle witnessing." Marveling at the uncanny beauty of a sunset or at the miracle of receiving help at the exact moment you needed it. Take a moment and think about a miracle that happened to you today. Were you feeling down and received an unexpected call from a loved one? Did you make it on time to an appointment even though you were running late? These are all moments of grace.

When you start living in the full reality of grace, you'll have an overwhelming sense of alignment. Everything you perceive will be in order. Your days will be a stream of miracle witnessing. It will become the constant state that you live in rather than a rare occurrence.

When you live in grace, you know that everything is working for you. You marvel at the divine order and synchronicity of not only everything around you, but also the *beyond* at play, that you can't necessarily see. In grace, you know that your inner and outer purposes are aligned with the divine, conspiring together. When you are living in grace, your worries about not getting what you want slip away because those worries are no longer being used as a crutch.

Stepping Into Grace

When you step into grace, you'll be able to surrender the outcomes of your desires, which is critical to their manifestation. To put in simple terms how this works, here's a blunt formula:

Desires = good

Attachment to their outcome = bad

While desires are the life force energy that's critical to your purpose, obsessing and worrying about whether or not they will happen will only work against you. Living in a state of grace, though, is how you release the negative attachment to outcome.

Let's talk a bit more about how it works before we dive into the lesson. Like so many of our soul purpose lessons, stepping into grace is at first about conscious intention. When you consciously invite and allow grace into your life, you'll begin to feel it. Eventually, it will just be your regular life experience.

When I first made a practice of consciously inviting grace into my life, I had moments when I would pause to admire the beauty of a tree or a sunset. I began taking in the presence of the world around me in a way I hadn't before, with reverence and wonder. I was able to attribute my spiritual condition to the presence of grace in my life each day.

There is nothing like the experience of grace when you are newly sober after being numb for so many years. However, as I started seeing and appreciating the daily miracles in my own life more regularly is when things really started to change. I would have regular experiences like bumping into someone on the street I hadn't seen in a long time who had an answer to something I was pondering. Or thinking about someone I hadn't spoken to in a while and then seeing them pop up in my social media feed. I started to notice what had always been there, but now, I marveled at it.

Practicing Grace = Conscious Surrender

There are a number of practices that may help you start living in the energy of grace, which is key to conscious surrender. Gratitude is a great way to experience grace. Noticing and giving earnest thanks for all the miracles that happen in your life every day. Or go deeper and make a list each day of 10 miracles that happened for you. Get specific about why they are miracles to acknowledge how the divine is taking care of you. The more you understand that you are deeply loved and taken care of, the less you feel the need to feel stress over getting what you want.

Another great way to experience grace is to practice observing the everyday miracles around you in nature. Sitting outside and witnessing how everything just magically works every minute of the day. Taking in with every essence of your being, the true wonder of the universe—how the planet orbits the sun perfectly, the sun rises and sets every day, things grow and die—will help you appreciate the energy of grace.

Live in The Energy of Grace

Why?

Grace is the key to surrendering all outcomes of what you want to the divine. The surrendering of all outcomes is key to your soul purpose journey. When we live in the energy of grace, there is no need to worry about outcomes. Because when we worry, what we're really saying is, "I'm not taken care of" or "I have to do it myself." All of these essentially amount to "I'm not going to get what I want." Which immediately blocks you from the flow of manifestation.

The Practice: Living in Grace

There are a few ways to experience living in grace. Like most spiritual practices, it starts with conscious intention. When you consciously invite the energy of grace into your life, you begin to experience more of it. The experience of grace is something that you can activate. Once activated, you can strengthen your experience with these practices.

What You'll Need

- Your journal
- A pen or pencil
- A quiet place where you can be fully present
- For the practice of observing nature, you'll need to be outside

How to Do It

There are a couple of different practices from which you can choose below. However, it's recommended you eventually incorporate all of them into your practice of experiencing grace. You should continue these as much as needed until you no longer need to "try" to experience grace. Once you are living in the energy of grace, you'll no longer need to practice invoking it. A great way to measure how well you are connected to grace will be how you react to the outcomes that are tied to your desires. Do you still fear not getting what you want or do you trust in the divine?

Step 1: Invite in the energy of grace into how you experience life. Each day, consciously invite grace into your life using the prayer below. You can implement this as a consistent part of your morning routine. As always, make sure you take a few deep breaths to center and ground yourself. Before you start this prayer, visualize your heart opening to receive these words.

I affirm that divine grace is how I experience the world. I ask the universe for its help and assistance in allowing me to experience the world as grace. That everywhere I look, I'll see miracles. That every single day I will witness the divine blessings that are happening for me. That I will live with deep, profound reverence for how much the universal consciousness loves me and is lovingly guiding me each step of the way. All is truly well. And so it is!

Step 2: Pick from the practices below and eventually incorporate all of them into your spiritual work. It's important that you *really feel* when doing these practices. Feel the wonder. Feel a sense of awe in your practice with each of these.

- **Gratitude List:** Being in gratitude is a great way to experience grace. If you don't already have a practice of gratitude, you should consider incorporating one. I recommend keeping a gratitude journal. When you list things you are grateful for, really feel it. Feel the inherent blessing in each.

- **Miracle List:** Similar to gratitude but with a slight twist is keeping a running list of miracles that happen to you each day. To do this, write at least 10 miracles that happen to you each day as well as your take on *why* they happened. Acknowledge why they are miracles. As with gratitude, be sure to feel each miracle deeply. Feel the wonder and gratitude deep in your heart for each of these blessings.

Miracles	Why it's a Miracle
I ran into Suzy unexpectedly.	Because I haven't seen her in years and she told me something I needed to hear.
I received an answer in my meditation.	I felt compelled to do a meditation today I haven't done in a while; when I did, it revealed to me the next chapter of my book.
My mom called me.	I was really feeling down and my mom called me when I needed to feel love.
I feel happy.	I woke up feeling sad but I started to think about everything I'm grateful for and how I feel happy. It's amazing how that works!
I ran for a couple miles.	I'm 43 and I've had knee issues and other health problems, yet my body continues to work for me and help me feel great.

- **Observe nature:** Observing the miracle that is nature is a great way to witness grace. How do birds fly with ease? The sun setting every day in all its glory. Practice really taking in nature with every essence of your being and feeling the wonder that comes with bearing witness to the marvel that is nature. Do this for just five to 10 minutes a day and you'll experience the energy of grace.

Spend as much time as you need on each of these practices. There is no timeline. You don't ever have to stop doing these practices. They will simply become a part of you and your way of being once you step into the energy of grace. You'll know you're living in the energy of grace when your fears begin to subside. Be patient with yourself. It's okay if it doesn't happen right away. In fact, that's normal. Just trust that with intention always comes a response.

CHAPTER 12

Love All Parts of You

"As you become more clear about who you really are, you'll be better able to decide what is best for you—the first time around."
- Oprah Winfrey

I t took me a long time to learn how to start loving myself. It's still a process and one I'm continually learning from. The greatest gift you can give yourself is the experience of really getting to know yourself and learning how to love each and every part of you.

When it comes to soul purpose, there is no greater lesson, as the very essence of living your soul purpose is about living a life that honors you. If you aren't clear who you really are or actively disavow and abuse certain parts of you, as I did and still sometimes do, it will be hard to do this wholly and completely.

My Road to Love

I've touched on parts of my story throughout this book. At the moment of writing this, I'm 43 years old and it was only recently that I learned how to start loving myself. A big part of that was a complete spiritual surrender, via getting sober, after struggling with addiction for most of my adult life. As part of this journey, I had to learn how to love who I am and let go of all the disappointment of who I'm not.

For me, I learned to doubt myself early on. I didn't have the tools to understand what it meant to express self-love and practice self-worth. As a result, I spent decades trapped in a cycle of self-abuse and disavowing who I really am. I didn't know how to sit with myself and be happy with what was there. All I knew was the need to escape. To escape what I felt, reality as I knew it, and ultimately, who I was.

As a result, I spent decades in the darkness. Literally. There was very little light in my life, though on the outside it appeared otherwise. I spent many years pretending that everything was okay. I was able to fool most into believing that it was, including myself. However, the search and the need for love of self was always there. So was the desire to be connected to something bigger than myself. Between each dark period of my life, there was always some part of me that was fighting for my divine essence, seeking to show it to me.

While my year of travel in 2011 was a pivotal point of my purpose journey, it was in also in the beginning of 2016 when the deepest part of my commitment to *self* truly began. I realized that I had been falling back into old patterns of self-abuse that were blocking me from manifesting my dreams. It was time to surrender to these. It was time to stop dabbling in finding my purpose, and instead to take a leap.

I started a business with a vision. Through this business I would find a way to align my heart with how I make money, no matter how long it took. The defining mantra that I repeated to myself each day, was *dare to believe*. This meant taking action toward believing that I could live each day with purpose, passion, and happiness. I decided that I was worth this, not just glimpses or moments, but a life every single day where soul purpose was a consistent, driving force in my life.

However, the truth is that even before this, I was always fighting for my soul and the expression of its purpose. Even at the times when that part of me lay dormant, upon reflection, I've come to realize that I was always daring to believe in my soul purpose. This includes when I:

- Quit my first job at 26 and moved to Los Angeles to pursue acting
- Moved to New York City because my inner guidance was pulling me there
- Allowed myself to travel a year with no worry or regret
- Left my last corporate job to start a soul purpose business

What became different in early 2016 is that I decided I was no longer going to merely dip my toes in the happiness pond or wait for it to come to me. I was going to love and honor myself enough to have it *be* my existence.

Practice of Self-Love

As part of this, I had to focus on bringing all the darkest parts of myself into the light. This included having an open, sincere look at the aspects of me that I didn't love, manifested in part as addiction. For me, addiction to alcohol was merely a symptom of a deeper story about a lack of self-love, not the story itself. Driven by a complete alignment with fear, AKA my ego, I eased my fears (particularly the ones tied to my dreams) though the abuse of alcohol. This toxic addiction disguised itself as therapy, allowing me to tolerate a life I didn't love for many years, too scared to make any real change and go after what I really wanted.

The beautiful thing is that enduring one of the most extreme forms of negative ego alignment, the disease of addiction, has allowed me to understand the depths of this spiritual challenge we all face to some degree. Namely, the human condition of ego. I used to just be grateful for the recovery from addiction, now I have the deepest gratitude for the experience of addiction itself.

As part of my recovery, I've had to have an honest look at that omnipresent voice that told me I wasn't smart enough, strong enough, lovable enough, pretty enough, thin enough, or talented enough. I had to look at all these parts and acknowledge them as a part of me, but not my truth. This is how I was able to move into authentic appreciation and reverence for me and begin to heal.

Through understanding where my lack of self-love came from, I was able to gain awareness of patterns that I no longer wanted to repeat. Through bringing them up into the light of day, I was able to see that they weren't the truth. In fact, the more I was able to accept who I am really am—light, love, a truly remarkable and wonderful person—I was able to start making decisions that reflected this. These choices led to a life worth living.

The key for me was to be gentle with myself. After years of being hard on myself, I knew this wasn't the answer. In fact, being hard gave me more of the same. We don't beat ourselves into spiritual shape, as often as we try to with other aspects of our lives. The spiritual practice of self-love requires patience, compassion, and understanding for self. When we can have true reverence for self, feeling the same sense of wonder that we feel when experiencing grace, do we begin a true and healing love affair with the most important relationship in our life, between you and yourself.

A continual practice of loving yourself is important to your soul purpose journey because this journey is synonymous with self-love. There is no soul purpose without self-love. Living your soul purpose is the greatest expression of self-love you will ever take on. One doesn't exist without the other. That's why I've reserved the most important lesson to your soul purpose journey for last.

Love All Of The Multifaceted Parts of You

Why?

The practice of self-love is inherent and deeply intertwined with your soul purpose journey. This includes learning to love ALL parts of you. For me, it meant loving the ego-aligned addict deep inside of me. As through learning to deeply cherish all your identities is how you practice self-love. It's a lifelong journey where you'll continually affirm and cradle yourself in the light and compassion of an all-encompassing love. Decide to be deeply in love with yourself and watch the magic of your soul purpose journey unfold.

The Practice: Write Yourself a Love Letter

While there are many self-love practices you can do, I've found that *writing yourself a love letter* is one of the most profound ways to build a loving relationship with yourself. It also helps to relax the ego, which is our self-created biggest critic. I've found that this works best when you allow yourself to free write. Don't think; just allow the words to flow. What is revealed will always offer a new insight that leads to greater self-love.

After doing these several times, I realized that my higher self was actually addressing my ego self. However, you don't need to set out with this intention. When beginning this practice, just write what comes and try to do so once a month.

What You'll Need

- Your journal

- A pen or pencil
- A quiet space that allows you to be fully present

How To Do It

From your quiet space and with an open heart and mind, follow these steps:

Step 1: Close your eyes and take several deep breaths in and out to center and ground yourself.

Step 2: Invite in divine love and guidance and set any intentions you have:

> *I now invite in the highest divine love to guide me in writing this letter for my highest good, self-love, and healing, according to divine will. I intend that whatever needs to be revealed for my own self-healing be shown through this process. And so it is!*

Step 3: Open your eyes and start writing. Write whatever comes out of your heart and flows onto the page. Here are some guidelines you can use if you wish:

- Express gratitude
- Be loving
- Ask for guidance where needed
- Be gentle

Step 4: I find it helpful to read the letter aloud several times over the weeks following. I always learn something new about myself that's critical to my own self-love process. When it feels time to write a new letter, do it.

Repeat this process as much as you want. I recommend once a month when you're first starting out. Know that self-love is a lifelong practice and there are many ways to enhance it. Most importantly, love the parts of you that are scared, angry, or sad as much as you love the more "positive" parts of you.

Your Journey

This book has been about my soul purpose story and the twelve lessons that have been absolutely essential to my journey. It's my profound hope that you find them as life-changing as I have and that they serve to completely upend your life for the better.

Please know that I'm on this journey with you. It's often said that we teach best what we most need to learn; this couldn't be more true for me[11]. In fact, in many ways, I'm only beginning. All of these lessons are ones I continue to practice, and at times even struggle with. Each continues to transform my life day by day:

- Lesson 1: Believe that you have a unique soul purpose.
- Lesson 2: Only your heart knows your soul purpose.
- Lesson 3: Ask the universe for what you want.
- Lesson 4: Surrender your deepest fears.
- Lesson 5: Release the limiting beliefs that bind you.
- Lesson 6: Believe in what you want with conviction.
- Lesson 7: Flow positive energy to your purpose.
- Lesson 8: Inspired action is the key to manifesting your soul purpose.
- Lesson 9: Let courage define you until it becomes you.
- Lesson 10: Release all forms of resistance.
- Lesson 11: Live in the energy of grace.
- Lesson 12: Love all of the multifaceted parts of you.

Know that as you embark on your journey, you might get discouraged. That's OK. It's your intention to evolve that matters,

---

[11] Betsy Morgan, Master Channel & Spiritual Teacher.

not your perfection of the lessons themselves, nor the end result. For me, some days are filled with moments of wonder and pure reverence for the synchronicities and daily miracles that *are* my life. Others are filled with frustration and even despair. I embrace them both. Both have value and represent opportunities for personal transformation. It's through our vulnerability that we grow the most. Therefore, know that the tough times are equally important to the empowered ones in *realizing* your soul purpose.

In fact, the greatest message I can leave you with is to reinforce that soul purpose is a ride; a beautifully exciting journey into the unknown. While this may feel like a scary proposition, pause and remember why you're doing this. Do you really want to continue living a life that only reflects a fraction of your true potential? Do you want to wonder *what if* or *what could have been*? Do you want to stay trapped in a life you don't love?

You don't.

I know how scary it can be to let go of everything you know and step into a new life. I truly do. And yes, it's never what you think it's going to be; sometimes it's worse, sometimes better. In the moments where the weight of my choice to pursue living my soul purpose feels particularly daunting, I remember something a close friend used to tell me in college. "Jessica," he'd say. "Think of life as a beautiful game. Have fun with it…Learn *the* game. Stop taking things so seriously."

Easier said than done, right?

However, what I realize is that he's 100% correct. It's this perspective that is the *key* to true happiness. To live in light, one must be light. Alternately, when we approach life from a place heaviness—a perspective of *finality* or *permanency*—this is what we experience in return. There isn't much room for change or growth here.

Therefore, bringing a playful energy into each of the lessons in this book will enhance your experience of them. Have fun with them and do your best to approach them as an opportunity to learn and grow. Focus less on what you want to get out of these lessons and more on *being* with them. Being present in your work, rather than focused on what you expect to reap, is how you'll receive the most value.

Additionally, allow yourself to be a student. We're all students in this life; I consider myself a student first and foremost. With this in mind, as you sit down each week, or day, to practice these lessons, allow yourself to feel curious and excited about what you will learn. In line with this, feel free to practice each lesson as much as you want, until you feel ready to move on, with no timetables or other rigid rules applied.

This is how I continue to approach them—finding the joy and wonder in what I continue to learn about myself, from a mindset of *fun*.

Make the Lessons Your Own

In line with bringing a playful reverence to these practices, make each lesson your own. If something doesn't feel right or isn't working for you, allow your intuitive guidance to adjust them. In short, make them your own. There's nothing to be afraid of in doing so. There is no such thing as "doing them right" or "messing them up." If your higher self is guiding you to take a different approach to any of the practices and steps in these lessons, listen and make any needed adjustments. In other words, your higher self is who is in charge here; not me, nor our collective ego. Always trust, listen, and follow your higher intuitive guidance in any spiritual work you do.

My Humble Honor

You have taken such a profound step towards greater happiness just by reading this book. You've decided to believe that your dreams are possible. Now, you embark on living them. Honor this in yourself.

For this and so much more, I thank you. I'm humbled and deeply honored that you have spent your precious time with me, reading about my story and taking to heart what I've learned along the way. Know that I will be waking up each day, sending you, and everyone who reads this book, my love, light, and the highest intention for your life.

You've got this. I believe in you.

Glossary of Terms

Soul purpose – An inner calling that is unique to you; it's what you've come here to do. It's not just about getting the things you want. It's a path that lights you up with such desire, intensity, and passion that it feels like a spiritual calling.

Ego self – An identity construct you've created to make sense of a physical world anchored in duality. It keeps you distinct and separate from the universal consciousness, which is love.

True self – Your divine essence, the spiritual *you*, that is one with God or divine presence. It exceeds your individual personality and is one with infinite consciousness.

The divine – The universal energy of consciousness, love, that *is* creation itself and connects us all. Some call it God, Source, higher power, or source energy. It is the loving guidance that is always there, all around and in us; It is us.

Limiting beliefs – Beliefs you've created based on false perceptions of yourself, life events or reality itself, anchored in fear.

Grace – The experience of awakening to the unconditional love that is always around you, expressed as gratitude, blessings and miracles that occur when you are in harmony with the divine.

Law of attraction – Anchored in the idea that *like attracts like*; your thoughts and feelings are considered to be powerful tools of co-creation.

Acknowledgements

This book wouldn't be possible without the love, help and support of the many people who worked on it with me.

Jasmine, your beautiful editing, thoughtful suggestions, and pushing me to dig deeper on my story of addiction, were essential to its completion.

Josh, your designs and creativity for the book cover and other artwork perfectly encapsulate everything I wanted to communicate.

Elaine, your continual belief in me and gentle nudges to *dare to believe*, were the spark I needed.

Bhakti, there would be none of this without you. Your love, support and incredible work on the marketing, production and *everything else*, were not only the backbone, but the fire.

Of course, none of this would be possible with the many friends and family members who have supported me throughout the years. The list is long, but you know who you are. I love each of you more than you can possibly imagine.

I want it to be known that every single one of my immediate family members has my love. I wouldn't be who I am without each of you.

Finally, I thank the *divine* for your endless guidance and love.

About the Author

Jessica Joines is on a mission to awaken every single person on the planet to their unique soul purpose and arm them with the tools to live it.

As an author, coach and inspirational speaker, she helps people master the 12 lessons that helped her discover what she already knew at the soul level: We are never destined to suffer. We are here to pursue our dreams.

With an honest, vulnerable yet straightforward approach, Jessica teaches people how to uncover and embrace their calling, through breaking down the spiritual principles, which led to her own awakening. The "DIY coursework" she's created is not only practical, but life altering. Her teachings are accessible and easily adopted by people from every walk of life.

Jessica's primary teaching is that of breaking through the illusion of fear and aligning to love, which is the lesson, she believes we all come here to learn.

For more information about upcoming classes, coaching and events, visit www.JessicaJoines.com

Made in United States
North Haven, CT
13 March 2025